PRAISE FOR *WHY SIN*

T0267704

"Released just two months
intimate and moving releas_ ___ _____
reiterates the lasting impact she left behind. If you're looking for creative context and thoughtful criticism of the media's role in O'Connor's personal and creative well-being, *Why Sinéad O'Connor Matters* is an essential read." — *American Songwriter*

"A revealing reappraisal . . . McCabe skillfully renders the artist's rise and ahead-of-her-time activism against the sociopolitical landscape of the 1980s and '90s, persuasively rescuing O'Connor's reputation from a mainstream media narrative that 'all too often dismissed [her] as a slow-motion train wreck.' Fans will be riveted." — *Publishers Weekly*

"A very personal and thought-provoking account of the media's role in O'Connor's stratospheric rise and ultimate implosion. . . . A touching tribute. O'Connor has been the subject of recent and numerous articles, a documentary, and books (including her own), but McCabe's take is unique in its critical analysis of the media and its attempts to silence and cancel O'Connor." — *Library Journal*

"*Why Sinéad O'Connor Matters* reassesses the oft-misunderstood songwriter and activist through a lens that is both historical and personal. . . . McCabe's impassioned defense of O'Connor in the wake of her many controversies is both heartfelt and persuasive." — *Aquarium Drunkard*

"Part biography, part reflection on the meaning of O'Connor's artistry and actions, McCabe traces the achievements and media-generated scandals of O'Connor's career, and how she consistently sought to beat her own path in a culture that condemned women for veering off the course of sanctioned archetypes. . . . What's most powerful is how McCabe draws on her own experience in parallel with O'Connor's. Perhaps this is O'Connor's most powerful asset as an artist: she opens up a space for people to see their struggles, their resistance and their trauma, in hers." — *The Irish Times*

"A superb showcase of the artist as a musician and a person. . . . The heart of this immaculate work lies in how McCabe deftly navigates the turbulent intersection of criticism and compassion. When McCabe talks transparently about her own childhood traumas and how they often mirrored O'Connor's, her candor is both refreshing and admirable. . . . This book sets a new standard in music criticism." — *Treble*

"A beautiful and compassionate meditation on silence, trauma, healing, and much more." — KCRW

"When people ask why I enjoy reading music criticism, I tell them the books shine a light upon our collective human psyche. *Why Sinead O'Connor Matters* by Alyson McCabe does exactly that. . . . The heart of this immaculate work lies in the intersection of criticism and compassion crafted by McCabe." — *Ancillary Review of Books*

"*Why Sinéad O'Connor Matters* is a thought-provoking look at one of the most influential artists and activists of our time that ultimately asks, 'Why did we abandon her?' In her time of need, when she needed support, when she stood by her values—her audience trusted the industry more than the artist. I hope this book is read by those who don't know Sinéad's story, and those that do will gain insight into the pain and punk ethos she still stands for. Allyson McCabe makes us all want to ask Sinéad for forgiveness and, one hopes, ask ourselves how we can do things differently."—Sharon Van Etten

"Allyson McCabe's intensely engaging, thoroughly researched, and deeply personal critical assessment, *Why Sinéad O'Connor Matters*, makes a serious and sharply observed yet compassionate appraisal of its subject, inarguably among the most influential artists of the late 1980s and early '90s. McCabe's willingness to reassess her own dismissal of Sinéad's work as being too pop to take seriously is rare; not many writers are willing to be honest about what they miss. Acknowledging that Sinéad's life story can be a difficult, contradictory mess, McCabe painstakingly relates this magnificent, irreplaceable artist's tale to her own heartfelt story, showing us in the process how and why so many of us also connect with Sinéad." —Vernon Reid

"Absolutely brilliant, heartbreaking, insightful, and personal."—Margo Price, *Literary Hub*

"Sinéad O'Connor is a brilliant, fragile, and exceptionally courageous talent whilst blessed with the voice of an angel. This book underscores why O'Connor, having been treated so carelessly by the world, remains relevant, and it treats her with the reverence she so rightly deserves."
—Shirley Manson

WHY
SINÉAD
O'CONNOR
MATTERS

Music
Matters

Evelyn McDonnell

Series Editor

WHY SINÉAD O'CONNOR MATTERS

Allyson McCabe

UNIVERSITY OF TEXAS PRESS

AUSTIN

Requests for permission to reproduce material from this work should be sent to
permissions@utpress.utexas.edu.

♾ The paper used in this book meets the minimum requirements of ANSI/NISO Z39.48-1992 (R1997) (Permanence of Paper).

Library of Congress Cataloging-in-Publication Data
Names: McCabe, Allyson, author.
Title: Why Sinéad O'Connor matters / Allyson McCabe.
Other titles: Music matters.
Description: First edition. | Austin: University of Texas Press, 2023. | Series: Music matters
Identifiers: LCCN 2022038478 (print) | LCCN 2022038479 (ebook)
    ISBN 978-1-4773-3073-9 (paperback)
    ISBN 978-1-4773-2571-1 (pdf)
    ISBN 978-1-4773-2572-8 (epub)
Subjects: LCSH: O'Connor, Sinéad—Criticism and interpretation. | O'Connor,
Sinéad—Influence. | Women rock musicians—Biography. | Women singers—
Biography.
Classification: LCC ML420.O297 M33 2023 (print) | LCC ML420.O297 (ebook) | DDC
782.42166/092 [B]—dc23/eng/20220817
LC record available at https://lccn.loc.gov/2022038478
LC ebook record available at https://lccn.loc.gov/2022038479

doi: 10.7560/325704

To all the Sinéads

CONTENTS

PROLOGUE

One day, I was looking for a music video on YouTube when I glanced off to the side of my search results at a thumbnail that read, "Mix: Fiona Apple cover of The Whole of the Moon—Live version."[1] I've often heard this song, written by Mike Scott in the mid-1980s, described as a tribute to exceptional, inspirational artists. That reading seems plausible, especially if you consider its most often quoted lyric: "I saw the crescent/But you saw the whole of the moon."

The same goes for Scott's up-tempo arrangement, with its strings, horns, synths, and relentlessly exuberant backup singers. There's even the sound of a blazing comet thrown into the proceedings. If you're a music nerd like me, you'll probably point out that Scott processed a BBC-sourced fireworks sound effect through an echo machine to create it . . .[2] But if you listen closely to the lyrics of the song's first chorus you might pick up on a different possibility: "You were in the turnstiles / With the wind at your heels / You stretched for the stars / You know how it feels / To reach too high / Too far / Too soon / You saw the whole of the moon."

Now maybe you think I'm reading too much into this. You think it's a good tune, and frankly you're kind of pissed that I'm being so intense about it. But if you're curious, you're probably going to click on that Fiona Apple link.

If you do, you'll likely discover that she isn't just covering an homage to some cool, creative people. Apple's face is animated by flashes of sorrow, passion, bitterness, and rage. Her voice is hoarse, and at times it sounds as though it might break.

But it actually gets stronger; she's gathering force as she goes. She moves around the mic like a boxer. The lyrics sheet is trembling in her hands. "I was dumb-found-ed by truth, YOU CUT THROUGH LIES . . ." Now she's pounding out the beat, stomping away with her feet. Then, as the music fades down, she looks up and smiles, breaks into a jig, and drops to the floor, knowing that she's crushed it.

But what exactly is "it" that she's crushed? For clues, you will see a link to yet another video. Click it and there is Fiona Apple again, this time with her laptop propped open on her bed, watching a video of Sinéad O'Connor performing "Mandinka" at the 1989 Grammys.[3]

From a technical point of view, this isn't exactly Queen at Live Aid. For one thing, it's an obvious lip sync. For another, O'Connor is slightly out of time with the music. And if you look closely, there's not even a band onstage. But none of this matters. Apple is totally rocking out with O'Connor, bopping her head in time. Now they're lip-syncing together, "I don't know no shame / I don't feel pain / I can't see the flame!"

At this point Apple stops lip-syncing to the video and cranks the volume way up. She watches the rest of the performance in silence and awe, then she kisses the screen. When the song is over, she applauds excitedly and summons her dog, to whom she raves, "I know! She's the fucking best! She's our hero!"

I can feel myself getting caught up in that energy, so I click on a video to the right of this one. Apple appears once more. It's only moments later, but this time she is looking off to the side of the camera. In a sad, serious tone she says, "Hello, Sinéad O'Connor. I'm Fiona Apple. I want you to know that you are my hero."[4]

What just happened? Apple explains that she has just seen a very different video of O'Connor, this one not a triumphant performance. She doesn't describe it explicitly, but it's clear from the context that she's referring to a twelve-minute monologue made nearly thirty years after O'Connor's Grammy appearance. Posted on Facebook in 2017 from a New Jersey Travelodge where O'Connor was living, it's a raw display of loneliness and anguish. O'Connor wipes away tears as she looks into the camera, talking about suffering from mental illness and struggling with thoughts of ending her life.[5]

"I don't want you to feel like that," Apple says, responding to O'Connor's pain. She affirms that O'Connor has given so much, tells her how much she wishes she could be with her, and that she is a friend. "That's all I want to say," Apple says, "You're my hero." The video ends abruptly.

Now I realize I haven't just been clicking on videos. I've been getting closer to the heart of my own story, which reaches back for generations. You see, I understand what it means to crush it, and to nearly be crushed by it.

My mother grew up in a South Philadelphia neighborhood that was once called Devil's Pocket, named by a local priest who said the kids there were so tough, they'd steal a dollar from the Devil's pocket.[6] That place became a part of her. After marrying my father and moving across town, she lived in his shadow, just as she had lived in the shadow of her father before him. It was a dark, dangerous shadow, and as a child I learned to fear it.

My father suffered from "demons," voices inside his

head that ignited violence, seemingly from thin air. My mother turned a blind eye to his abuse, or told me I must have done something to set him off. And his fists were nothing compared to the belt her father used to beat her, so what made me so special, anyhow?

I wasn't so special. But I was different—too small, too smart, too self-aware for her, and, I feared, for the world. So I pretended not to give a fuck about anything, but I felt everything—deeply, maybe too deeply. And I knew that most of my feelings were not okay . . . especially not the queer ones, the one that made me feel like a boy who liked girls rather than a girl who liked boys. I sublimated my alienation and self-loathing into dreams of future rock-'n'-roll badassery, ideas I took largely from the radio and television.

My best and only friend T had MTV, so we'd cut high school together, get stoned at her apartment, and watch music videos. All those leather straps, safety pins, and zippers; pure flash and swagger. I fantasized about slinging my guitar way down low like my outlaw heroes and escaping to the other side of the screen, where another life awaited me.

Too freaked out to actually try to become that person, I cut my hair into a spiky mullet and piled on black kohl eyeliner, splitting the difference between Joan Jett and Chrissie Hynde. Next came a few false starts at a commuter school and then a mind-numbing data entry job. Then, in 1991, I made a miraculous landing at Hampshire College, an upside-down planet where the oddballs, misfits, and weirdos were the cool kids.

It was there I met my first girlfriend, read Michel Foucault and Judith Butler, and discovered entirely new musical worlds: hip-hop, trip-hop, and a new sound called "grunge." One of my roommates even turned me on to queer artists. Who even knew there was such a thing?

I got way into Phranc, but not Cris. I loved Two Nice Girls, but not The Indigo Girls, k.d. lang, Melissa Etheridge, Tracy Chapman, or anyone who sounded even remotely MOR to my angry young ears. Campus lore had it that Chumbawamba once crashed in our on-campus apartment before "Tubthumping," when they were still a legit anarcho-communist punk band. The Riot Grrrl scene was still in its infancy thousands of miles away, not on my radar for at least a few more years.

As for Sinéad O'Connor, like the rest of the world, I was well aware of who she was thanks to her 1990 MTV megahit "Nothing Compares 2 U." But if she failed to land for me, it was because by then I had categorically renounced pop music, which I defined as any song with any airplay on any station on any airwaves anywhere.

Even after her infamous 1992 appearance on *SNL*, I probably saw her as indistinguishable from Michelle Shocked or Ani DiFranco, or any of the local queer-adjacent folkies playing in the coffeehouses in and around Northampton, Massachusetts. On campus, virtually every girl, including my roommate, had a shaved head and combat boots. If you wanted to be radical there, you had to do a lot more than tear up a photo of the pope.

Throughout graduate school, my academic career, and my early years as a music journalist, my views of O'Connor remained largely unchallenged. Everything I thought I knew about her was determined by nonstop tabloid headlines. She's married, she's divorced, ditto, ditto, ditto, ditto. She's come out as a lesbian, nope, not anymore. She's been ordained as a Catholic priest. Whoops, she's now a Muslim. You can call her Magda Davitt. Scratch that, it's Shudada Sadaqat. She's been diagnosed as bipolar. No, it's actually borderline personality disorder. And/or PTSD. Actually, all of her mood swings are the result of her hysterectomy. Oh, and did I mention that Prince once beat her up, and that Arsenio Hall was his drug dealer? Tune in. You can see it all today on *Dr. Phil.*

I had no idea that O'Connor had remained creatively prolific, releasing nearly a dozen solo albums in addition to many singles, songs made for films, collaborations with other artists, and appearances at live charity events. I didn't know that many of the public statements she made were lucid and insightful, and that when she called bullshit, she often got it right, especially about the important stuff.

She was right about the role of the Catholic Church in condoning and covering up child abuse. She was right about the music industry's fixation on defining success in purely commercial terms. She was right about its racism, and the way it uses and silences women, pimping them out when they're young and abandoning them when they're not. Most of all, she was right to seek and speak her own truth, even though she's paid — and continues to pay — a terrible price for it.

Recent reckonings, such as those facilitated by the #MeToo and Time's Up movements, underscore that O'Connor's fame as a global pop star peaked in the early 1990s.[7] There was virtually no public discourse around mental health, and no understanding of how the public expression of pain connects to trauma. At the same time, paparazzi, gossip rags, and salacious talk shows made millions by destroying women. There were few mechanisms to help women tell their own stories, control their own messaging, or clap back against misogynist misrepresentation.

Consequently, trauma was too often perpetuated and compounded by the media, and perpetrators weren't held to account. Even when women spoke out, their outcries were often weaponized against them, used as further ammunition to take them down or turn them into punch lines.

For me, following the links in those Fiona Apple videos turned out to be only the starting point. As I came to a deeper understanding of how this problematic framing obscured the way I'd seen O'Connor, as well as the way I had experienced and understood the trajectory of my own life, I started to consciously dismantle it. As part of that work, I went back and reexamined O'Connor's interviews and public statements over the years, and listened closely to her songs again, this time hearing her for the first time, and tuning into everything I had missed previously.

Sometimes when I told people what I was doing, they gave me eye rolls, or they would come right out and ask, "Isn't she nuts?" Other times they flat out asked me if *I* was nuts, which was hurtful, but every time that happened, I dug in. It felt like the only way to understand where all this shaming was coming from and, more importantly, how to overcome it.

I initially thought of what I was doing as taking a look back at an artist who had left the public stage after her 2017 Facebook post and subsequent disastrous appearance on *Dr. Phil.* But in 2020, O'Connor quietly reentered public life with a string of sold-out US shows, mostly in small venues along the West Coast.

As a New Yorker, I didn't have the chance to see her

perform, although I had access to social media posts and YouTube clips showing that she was still radiant. When I heard that she planned to extend and expand her tour to coincide with the thirtieth anniversary of *I Do Not Want What I Haven't Got*, I thought I'd finally have my chance. But those plans were paused by the pandemic, and then I read that O'Connor had entered a one-year intensive rehab program for trauma and addiction, derailing her tour plans indefinitely.

Once again, it looked like it was the end of O'Connor's story. But then, shortly after she entered treatment, another announcement went out that she was finishing a memoir to be published in summer of 2021. I got my hands on an advance review copy of her book, devoured it, and pitched a profile to NPR.

If you've never heard my stories before, I should explain that I don't do two-way interviews that hew closely to talking points, much less anything that sounds like a standard arts news report. I see the peg (the industry term for why we're covering this book/album/film) as a jumping-off point for something far more substantive than a headline plus summary or review.

Though I may only have a few brief minutes on air, I try to use every second of narration, interviews, archival material, and the artist's work to craft a minidocumentary with a broader public point. I'm one part culture reporter, one part culture remixer. I'm on a mission to move the dial so the "why" is set to a deeper understanding of what's at stake.

When I got the green light from "Morning Edition," my plan was for O'Connor to more or less tell her own story. I hoped to desensationalize the profile so that it wasn't just "Remember that crazy bald-headed woman who tore up a photo of the pope?" but "Remember the talented artist who was canceled for calling attention to something terrible that we all now know to be true?"

My story was broadcast on June 1, 2021, both the day O'Connor's memoir came out and my birthday.[8] I'm not superstitious about the coincidence, but I still wasn't quite done with the story, and it wasn't done with me. So now I offer you this expanded look at O'Connor's life and work through the lenses of music criticism, cultural analysis, and personal reflection. Consider this to be the "extended play" version, remastered with all the bits that never made it on the air for one reason or another.

To be clear, my reappraisal of O'Connor's significance isn't based solely on my "professional" ear as a music journalist, nor is this work intended to be regarded as a comprehensive biography — or an uncritical hagiography. Instead, I'm approaching the work as a chance to connect the dots and present things from a fuller and more nuanced perspective. Insofar as O'Connor's talents are inseparable from her struggles and triumphs, so are mine and yours.

FRAMING

Before I became a journalist, I was an academic cultural theorist. If you want to construct a scholarly argument, you cite other people. In journalism, it's basically the same. But whatever academics or journalists claim, no matter how many times we do it, no matter how committed we are to sticking to the facts, absolute certainty does not exist.

When I was transitioning out of teaching at Yale en route to my current vocation, I took a brief detour through a journalism graduate program. There was this one professor we used to call "Sarge," who was always blathering on about how the number-one rule of journalism was that you had to "get everything on record." As my classmates scribbled away in their notebooks, I interrupted him. "What does that mean — get it on record?"

Sarge was flummoxed. "It means pull out your goddamn notebook, McCabe, and write down everything the subject says. That way when they say later that they never said it, you can pull out that notebook and say, 'Yes, you did!' When they threaten to sue you, you can pull out that notebook and say, 'Go ahead, make my day!'"

Everyone nodded and laughed, scooping up Sarge's pearls of wisdom. "But who's to say they didn't just make up what they told you? Or that you didn't just make it up or distort what they said when you wrote it down?" I asked. "Then you get other people to talk to you," Sarge replied, clearly exasperated, "and get them on the goddamn record, too!"

Everything in my lived experience up to that moment led me to reject this position as stubbornly naïve, or absurd, the idea that THE TRUTH can be established through the steady accumulation of testimony, transcribed by a disinterested hand acting as judge and jury. Anyone who's ever done an interview knows it isn't a witness statement, and a memoir is even less so. Famous or not, people say the things they think other people want to hear and revise or hold back what they don't. Contradictions and omissions aren't simply a consequence of dissemblance or forgetting. They're the residue of feelings, not entirely erased, only obscured.

Those who can "read" this half-hidden ink aren't superhuman empaths who conceal their identities behind a mild-mannered facade to serve the noble cause of truth and justice. They're just better at understanding that the truth appears as much in what's not said as in what is, and in how it's said, and when and where, and to whom, and why. Tuning your ear is totally different than sharpening your pencil. It starts with being in touch with yourself and being willing to risk exposing your own vulnerability to see or hear what someone else is trying to tell you.

This may be especially true for musicians, music journalists, and ardent music fans — all of us searchers. Thankfully for us, the celestial jukebox is a limitless lost and found. Think about your favorite songs, especially the sad ones, and why they resonate for you so strongly. It's not necessarily the specific circumstances being described in the lyrics or the precise way the notes are arranged on the staff. Instead, it's in the imaginary conversation you're having with the artist, and how it helps you to connect in some way with your own experience.

That experience often indexes something you've lost, whether consciously or not. Songs can help us bring it back, recollect it, make sense of it, or at least learn how to live with its absence. Even though memory is never identical to the thing that's been lost, that doesn't mean we shouldn't try to remember. It means we should try harder. As time goes by, we may find ourselves further removed from one kind of truth (what it was) but edging ever closer to another (what it means).

Going into my interview with Sinéad O'Connor, I knew it wasn't going to be as easy as the interviews I've done before with artists such as Laurie Anderson, John Cale, or Thurston Moore—all big names and big talents, but not people I personally related to on the same level, not people whose music has made me weep so much or so deeply. I knew that O'Connor's story wouldn't be easy for me to tell, but that's why it felt especially important for me to try.

Although my profile would be built on my interview with O'Connor, to bring context to her story I also interviewed feminist punk icon Kathleen Hanna and music critic Jessica Hopper. When I started putting all of the tape together, I assumed that the hardest part was going to be packing everything I wanted to cover into five minutes of airtime.

Changing the narrative about O'Connor proved far more difficult. The main point of contention was over using tape from her 1992 *SNL* appearance.[1] Rather than leading with it, or bringing it in at all, I wanted the show host to refer to it only briefly in their introduction — something along the lines of:

> "Sinéad O'Connor rose to the top of the charts with an unforgettable song [Clip of 'Nothing Compares 2 U']. Two years later a controversial appearance on *Saturday Night Live* dimmed the limelight. But O'Connor is out now with a new memoir, and she says that moment re-railed — rather than derailed — her career." Allyson McCabe has the story.

Then, rather than reminding the audience that O'Connor was canceled, I wanted to show how and why she was canceled. That meant bringing in tape from Joe Pesci's appearance on *SNL* the week after hers.[2] Pesci goes after O'Connor aggressively in his three-plus minute monologue, at first referring to what happened fairly neutrally, as "an incident." He then tells the audience he thought tearing up the photo was wrong, and explains that he asked someone to paste it back together. He holds up the reassembled photo and the audience applauds wildly. "Case closed," Pesci says. But it wasn't.

Pesci went on to implicitly blame Tim Robbins, who had hosted the episode, for "the incident," for letting O'Connor get away with it. Then he remarked that she was lucky, "because if it was my show, I would have gave her such a smack." Pesci held his hand to demonstrate the smack, and, again, the crowd broke out in applause — accompanied by cheers. Pesci took it in, smiling from ear to ear. "I would have grabbed her by her . . . by her . . ."

This is where I wanted to abruptly cut the tape. The word Pesci says next is "eyebrows," a crack about O'Connor being bald, but of course the audience would hear the cut and think what he said was "pussy," and think of Donald Trump. And that is exactly what I wanted them to think. My point wasn't that Pesci = Trump. I know that Pesci was reciting lines he probably didn't write and expressing wiseguy viewpoints he may or may not have actually felt.[3]

What I wanted to show with my tape cut was that Pesci's lines landed because the audience felt them. The point was not that he was a misogynist. It was that the audience, and by extension the larger culture, was misogynist.

In using that tape cut, I hoped to pose an implicit question: To what extent did misogyny mediate the way we saw O'Connor in 1992? And to what extent is it still woven — consciously and unconsciously — into our cultural scaffolding? This isn't just a matter of perspective, male versus female. As a journalist, I've worked with men who acknowledge misogyny as a problem, and women who don't. When it seeps into reporting it's rarely overt — which is what makes it so powerful, and so hard to fight.

In this case, my editor (at that time) was a middle-aged cisgender heterosexual white man who would certainly identify himself as feminist. Nevertheless, he used words and phrases like "too suggestive" and "overkill" to urge me to dial Pesci down and bring more of O'Connor's "incident" in for "balance." Which one of us was right?

On the one hand, journalists are supposed to be neutral: just the facts, ma'am. That's what we're taught and how we're trained. But deciding what tape to use and where to cut it are intentional choices with powerful ramifications. They deeply influence how we frame a story and give it context and meaning — and how you as the public see and hear it.

Therefore, our clash was more than a trivial difference of opinion. It was, on the contrary, a fundamental though unspoken disagreement. My editor wanted to include O'Connor's performance to remind listeners about the controversy that she invited or even provoked. I wanted to include Pesci's monologue to show how O'Connor was reprimanded and why.

Better, I think, for journalists to be transparent about these positions and to own them, rather than to pretend that one is objective and the other is biased. But deadlines are deadlines, especially in daily news, so rather than argue, I agreed to include brief clips from both tapes for "balance."

However, I pushed for a new title, so it was "Sinéad O'Connor Has a New Memoir . . . and No Regrets" rather than the one the editor had floated, in which she "proclaimed" that she has no regrets. I also landed on the point that what O'Connor won't do is apologize *for surviving*—which was far more suggestive than anything I would have been able to show with the tape cut.

In the end, I think my title reflected the main point of the story, but it wasn't the whole story. Even if I had five years instead of five minutes, it would have been impossible to present a comprehensive biography. O'Connor explicitly denounced several unauthorized attempts in the early 1990s.[4] In 2012, she pulled out of a biography project that she had officially sanctioned after only six months.[5]

Even in her own 2021 memoir, O'Connor acknowledged that there are significant challenges in telling her own story, namely, that her recollections are riddled with inconsistencies, gaps in her memory that she attributes to not being present for large chunks of her life. She says other memories are private, or concern matters she would prefer to forget. In the foreword, she tells readers that she hopes her book will nevertheless make sense. If not, she advises us to "try singing it and see if that helps."[6]

I want to take that advice and honor it, to accept the inevitable gaps and inconsistencies, the difficulty of getting it right, and the impossibility of pure neutrality. I therefore plan not simply to recite O'Connor's story, but to "sing" it *bel canto*, which, as she explains in her memoir, has nothing to do with mastering scales, breathing, or any other formal technique.[7] Instead, it's about singing in your own voice, allowing your emotions to take you to the notes, and allowing the notes to take you to the truest expression of the song.

Such an approach entails not only close reading but telling O'Connor's story intimately, feeling the feelings myself, and letting the notes that are inside of me spill out onto the page from time to time, a bit like Fiona Apple's duet with O'Connor in the "Mandinka" YouTube video. My goal, simultaneously easier and more difficult than conventional biography, is to illustrate *why O'Connor matters*, and to ground that assessment in the circumstances of her life and work and in mine. As you read, I invite you to hold up a lighter, or a mirror, and sing along with us too, all of us piercing through the darkness together . . . journeying toward the kind of catharsis that only music can bring. Where better for us to begin than at the beginning?

TAKE 1

Sinéad Marie Bernadette O'Connor was born in Glen-ageary, County Dublin, Ireland, on December 8, 1966. She is the daughter of John (sometimes also known as Sean), an engineer who would go on to become a barrister, and Marie, a trained chef and dressmaker who would go on to become a homemaker. Sinéad is the third of the O'Connor's four children. The oldest is Joseph, a prize-winning novelist. Next is Eimear, an eminent art historian. The youngest is John, a psychotherapist. Sinéad is, of course, a musician who has sold millions of records worldwide. She has also been objectified, criticized, psychoanalyzed, hospitalized, sensationalized, and all too often dismissed as a slow-motion train wreck. How did all of this happen?

Let's start over, this time with another set of facts: the day of Sinéad O'Connor's birth falls on the Feast of the Immaculate Conception. In the Catholic theocracy of 1960s Ireland, this was a very big deal. The celebration of the Virgin Mary's sinless life was the unofficial start of the Christmas season. Schools were closed, the faithful flocked to Mass, and religious visions were reported all around the country.

O'Connor's parents chose her second middle name, Bernadette, in honor of Bernadette Soubirous, whose teenage sightings of the Virgin Mary led to her canonization as Our Lady of Lourdes. As a child, O'Connor says, she believed in the miracle too, proved when her grandmother splashed holy water from Lourdes on her foot, spontaneously curing a wart that would have otherwise necessitated surgery.[1]

All of this is to say Sinéad O'Connor was born and raised in the Catholic faith, which was not at all unusual for Irish kids of her generation. As she once explained, "If a bishop came walking down the street, people would move to make a path for him. If a bishop attended a national sporting event, the team would kneel to kiss his ring. If someone made a mistake, instead of saying, 'Nobody's perfect,' we said, 'Ah, sure, it could happen to a bishop.'"[2]

O'Connor's family was not perfect. In fact, they were deeply flawed, even horrifically flawed. Today, and certainly back then, most kids would keep that to themselves, not only because "nobody's perfect" but also because it feels too shameful to admit that to yourself, much less to the world. As any survivor will tell you, present company included, part of the psychology of abuse is that the victim is pulled into a code of silence created by the perpetrator, and made to believe that on some level they deserve to be abused, or that they are the troubled one.

They're told that they mustn't tell anyone, and that if they do, no one will believe them, and even if they are believed, the situation will only become worse once it's dragged out into the open. So if you are abused, as a survival strategy you become very good at hiding the evidence. If you want to live, mum's the word.

Sure, some people will still see the clues. O'Connor says the nuns at her school often wondered why her clothing was filthy, why she was starving, and where her bruises came from. Sometimes they asked, other times they suggested directly that her mother was the source. O'Connor says she denied the truth to protect her mother, and to protect herself from her mother's retaliation.[3] But from the very beginning of her public life as an adult, O'Connor has been unflinchingly honest about her upbringing, recounting experiences that are hard to hear—and that were no doubt much harder to endure.

She describes how, without provocation, her mother would erupt in violence almost daily, how she would make O'Connor strip and would beat her across her genitals, telling O'Connor that she wished she had never been born, that she hated that she was born a girl, and that she wanted to rip out O'Connor's womb. She made O'Connor beg for mercy, ordering her to repeat over and over again, "I am nothing . . ." until O'Connor felt like nothing.[4]

Afterward, O'Connor says her mother would often lock her away in a room or in the space beneath the stairs. Where was her father in all of this? Once, in her memoir, she says he broke down a door and took her to a doctor, clearly upset by the sight of blood on her face. But he didn't say much about it then, or later, or even when the police came to their house following up on calls placed by concerned neighbors who had heard the sounds of screaming.

He, like the others in the O'Connor household, obeyed the code of silence. No one said a word to the police for fear that they would and could do nothing, and that as soon as they left, the beatings would resume, maybe even more viciously. When she was being beaten, O'Connor says she would sometimes see Jesus, picturing Him on a cross on a little stony hill, promising to restore the blood her mother had taken from her with His own blood, which would make her heart strong and allow her to survive.

At that time, the Catholic Church was strongly opposed to divorce, and it was explicitly prohibited by the Irish Constitution. Yet O'Connor's father still left when she was seven or eight. Sinéad says her mother was so distraught that she banished the kids to the backyard, where they lived for weeks in a shed that their father had built for their amusement.

O'Connor's mother once became so enraged when she noticed a button missing from Sinéad's hand-me-down dress that she locked Sinéad away in a dark room and took her siblings on a weekend trip to a friend's house. Scared and alone, and confined for days without food, O'Connor says she prayed to God, pledging her undying devotion if He would save her.

In a way, O'Connor's prayers came true. Six years later her father won full custody of the children, something of a miracle in a country where the courts sided almost invariably with mothers in cases of separation, and divorce would not be legalized until a decade later. Though the ruling must have seemed like a miracle, it could not undo thirteen years of abuse and neglect, thirteen years with no functional parenting in her life. By the time O'Connor came to live with her father, she was running wild in the streets, skipping classes, shoplifting, and stealing from strangers. She was expelled from at least three schools and hauled into police stations seven or eight times.

There is a lot about this story that rings true for me. I'm four years younger than O'Connor, and I grew up far from the dictates of the Church. Still, I knew a lot of girls just like her, girls who sold dollar joints out of their school lockers, girls who got into churchyard fistfights because someone looked at them the wrong way, girls who had problems with authority because they had experienced only arbitrary, senseless, or ruthless authority or because they had experienced no authority at all.

I really want to tell you that I was not one of those girls. That I had better or knew better. But the truth is that when I was in my teens I ran wild too. I ran from my father's rages, from my mother's silences and indictments, and, most of all, from myself. I often succeeded in outrunning the shadow, but every once in a while, it would catch up with me.

When I was in grad school in my mid-twenties, I took a documentary film class. The professor dimmed the lights and started screening cinema verité pioneer Frederick Wiseman's *High School*. As in all of Wiseman's films, there is no narration, only the camera's eye guiding the audience toward certain interpretations. One scene showed teachers pointing out the physical imperfections of the female contestants during a school-run fashion show. Another showed a teacher bullying a male student into putting on his gym uniform, sternly warning him, "You don't talk! You just listen!"

Wiseman filmed his documentary in black and white, at the height of the Vietnam War, and in the months leading up to the 1968 student uprisings in Paris. He might have seen the high school as a site of conflict between conformity and rebellion, an ideological battleground where discipline took the place of education. That is certainly how my grad school classmates saw it. But I had a different perspective.

As the opening scene started rolling, I was startled to see

Wiseman's camera cutting a path through the neighborhood where I grew up in Northeast Philadelphia, through the alleyways behind the houses, past the shabby laundry that had been left out on the line to dry, then literally down my block, then past the craft supply store where T and I met when we were both hired to sort through stock in the filthy, wet basement, then to the high school we hardly attended.[5]

I had no idea that this film was ever made, or that it was banned from being shown in Philadelphia.[6] Twenty years after it was released, the draconian rhetoric it captured was no more effective or relevant than Nancy Reagan's War on Drugs. By then the school was more akin to a factory than a prison, and there were thousands of students aimlessly roaming the austere cinder-block hallways, far too many for teachers to even try to control. Theoretically, rule violations led to detentions, detentions led to suspensions, and suspensions led to expulsions, but when school administrators failed to make good on these threats, I simply stopped going.

My mother's signature was easily forged on absence notes, and even easier was checking in at morning homeroom then ducking out a side door to meet up with T, who lived right across the street. Her mother worked all the time, and there was no dad around, so we'd hang out at her apartment or hop on the bus to the El to South Street, where we'd lurk in the famous punk shops, hit up strangers for money to buy cigarettes and booze, and have our fortunes read by our favorite psychic, Mrs. Oliver.

No one ever asked us what we were doing in the streets in the middle of the school day. If they had, we would have just laughed at them and run. We were always running from something, running away from all the feelings we couldn't talk about. This was our sad version of freedom: running from a truth that no one understood or cared enough to help us escape.

Not so for Sinéad O'Connor. On the advice of social workers, her father placed her in the care of nuns at An Grianán, a residential reform school for girls operated by the Catholic Church and funded by the Irish Department of Education. In their worst days, reform schools like An Grianán took babies away from their teenage mothers shortly after their births. Decades later, mass graves were discovered on the grounds with tombstones bearing only the name "Magdalene."[7]

By the time O'Connor arrived at An Grianán in the 1980s, these secret, shameful practices were largely discontinued, with the last of the teenage girls now elderly women living out their lonely final years in a hospice on the school's grounds. But O'Connor still describes her own experience there as "Dickensian."[8]

She says girls at the school were kept under strict lock and key, and made to feel unwanted by their families. As punishment for infractions of the school's policies they were forced to sleep on the hospice floor amid the wails and moans of the dying women; and in place of education, they had to wash the priest's frocks with cold water and bar soap in a basement laundry. The rationale for all of this harshness was to instill discipline, to set the wayward girls on a righteous path toward salvation.

O'Connor was smart and cheeky and, after nearly two years at the school, not the least bit reformed. But her life did turn around when one of the nuns, Sister Margaret, gave O'Connor her first guitar, arranged for her to have lessons, and bought her a red parka she coveted from No Romance, a punk shop in Dublin. More than that, Sister Margaret gave O'Connor the love she never received from her own mother.

O'Connor says Sister Margaret didn't love her despite the fact that she was rebellious, but rather *because* she was rebellious.[9] She encouraged her to follow her dreams and to know that God was always with her. Now, if this were a movie, O'Connor would have immediately won over the other nuns with her extraordinary gifts. They would have softened their repressive grip, maybe even staged their own musically scored liberation, something like a campy mash-up of *Sister Act* and *Riverdance*.

But of course that's just as ridiculous as Jim Forbes's assertion in *Behind the Music* that O'Connor taunted the nuns by repetitively performing "House of the Rising Sun" (the title of which is a rough translation of "An Grianán").[10] Though O'Connor didn't refute Forbes then, she said years later that she would have been far too scared to have pulled a stunt like that.[11] I believe it's far more likely that the nuns put up with her music because they knew she needed an emotional outlet, or simply because they couldn't deny the incredible, almost supernatural quality of her voice.

I reject the idea that O'Connor's abuse was somehow "for a reason" or "all part of God's plan." But I can see how music became an emotional balm for this small doe-eyed girl who had survived so much darkness, and held so much fight inside with nowhere to put it until she found her voice. To quote Saint Augustine, "Anger is the first step toward courage."

For O'Connor, the next was waiting just beyond the

walls of the school. As O'Connor neared the end of her time at An Grianán, her guitar teacher invited her to perform at her wedding. O'Connor was so nervous singing Barbra Streisand's "Evergreen" that her knees knocked together the whole time. But that didn't stop her from impressing the bride's brother, Paul Byrne.

Byrne happened to be the drummer in a band called In Tua Nua, whose connections with U2 ran deep.[12] Bandmate Vinnie Kilduff had played uilleann pipes and bodhrán on U2's 1981 album *October*. Steve Wickham played the fiddle on their breakout 1983 hit "Sunday Bloody Sunday." When U2 founded Mother Records as a one-off singles label to promote other Irish artists, it was In Tua Nua that it tapped first.

Byrne was so moved by O'Connor's singing that he invited her to join In Tua Nua. She co-wrote her first song, "Take My Hand," for the band; its lyrics were inspired by a night she spent in punishment on the floor of the hospice at An Grianán.[13]

But O'Connor was too young to go on tour, so she was soon replaced by a different vocalist, Leslie Dowdall, who sang on the band's 1984 single "Coming Thru," which became Mother's first release. After it became a big radio hit in Ireland, In Tua Nua got a deal with Island Records.

Although the band's unique combination of rock, modern folk, and traditional Irish music put it on track for commercial success, several members departed in quick succession. O'Connor transferred to a less restrictive Quaker boarding school and performed with bands such as The Waterboys on occasion, although at fifteen she was still too young to tour extensively.[14]

After getting arrested for performing in a pub underage, O'Connor quit school altogether and moved to Dublin's gritty Temple Bar neighborhood, where she got by through busking, waitressing, and delivering kiss-o-grams in a French maid costume while waiting for her next big break. She didn't have to wait long.

Since the mid-'70s, Ireland had been a fertile proving ground for bands such as Thin Lizzy, Stiff Little Fingers, The Undertones, The Boomtown Rats, and The Vipers. The early '80s saw the rise of artists such as U2 and Dexys Midnight Runners, the latter of which—despite coming out of the British punk scene—scored a massive pop hit with "Come On Eileen," thanks to its Celtic strings. The Waterboys, The Pogues, Hothouse Flowers, and My Bloody Valentine would soon become part of this ongoing "Irish invasion."

In the summer of 1984 O'Connor found her next outfit, Ton Ton Macoute, by placing an ad in *Hot Press*, the Irish analogue to *Rolling Stone*. She didn't share bass guitarist Colm Farrelly's enthusiasm for witchcraft and mysticism, but at least he agreed to let O'Connor sing some of her own songs rather than just tired rock-'n'-roll covers. Their acoustic funk band quickly built a local following, earning them a chance to perform at a showcase for London-based Ensign Records, which had recently been acquired by label powerhouse Chrysalis.

Ensign's cofounder Nigel Grainge had already signed some of the highest-profile Irish acts, including The Boomtown Rats, who had scored their first Top 40 hit on the UK singles chart with "Lookin' After #1" less than a year into their recording contract, and The Waterboys, whose 1983 self-titled debut made waves in the United Kingdom with the single "A Girl Called Johnny." Grainge didn't think Ton Ton Macoute was anywhere close to that league, but he saw O'Connor's potential and invited her to keep in touch. She told him she was writing lyrics and asked whether he would be interested in hearing them if she were able to turn them into songs. "Sure," he said, even sending her a plane ticket.

A few months later, Sinéad O'Connor's estranged mother was driving to Mass when her car skidded on an icy road, resulting in a fatal crash. O'Connor says she was enraged at the people who turned up at the funeral and knew her family but did nothing to help them—and at her father, who cried and prayed over her mother's casket, apologizing over and over to his ex-wife, but not to the children who had suffered at her hand. O'Connor cried like a baby at the funeral, then she ran.

There are a few different versions floating around about what happened next, but to me this is the one that rings the most emotionally true: a few weeks later, O'Connor hopped on a plane to London and phoned Grainge from the airport.[15] "Where should I go for that demo session?" she asked. Grainge was flustered, only barely remembering that he had made her the offer. As a courtesy, he sent her to a studio, where she met with Karl Wallinger, who had recently left The Waterboys to form World Party. After they worked out a few songs together, Wallinger called Grainge and said, "You might want to come by for a listen."

When he arrived, they were in the middle of recording a song called "Troy," a hauntingly mesmerizing account of love and betrayal, set in a lush bed of symphonic strings. O'Connor's voice shifts from sorrow to fury and back again, referencing the slaying of dragons, the rising of the phoenix from the flame.

One of the lines in the refrain, "There is no other Troy

for you to burn," was drawn from W. B. Yeats's poem "No Second Troy." It was published in 1916 for his beloved Maud Gonne, a revolutionary for Irish independence and women's rights, who had shattered him by spurning his affection.

The other lyrics were of O'Connor's invention—interpreting Yeats through the lens of her own experience. At first, she sings from the perspective of the abuser telling the aggrieved that she never meant to hurt her, but then O'Connor shifts to lines delivered with such palpable anger, they seemed to be spit by fire:

> I have learned I will rise
> And you'll see me return
> Be what I am
> There is no other Troy for me to burn

As the song's intensity built toward its close, you could hear her sing over and over again, "You're still a liar," but it sounded quite a bit like "You're still alive." Grainge didn't know where all of this passion came from. He didn't know much about O'Connor at all. But he did know that the eighteen-year-old had all the makings of a superstar, so he signed her on the spot.

THE LION AND THE COBRA

To grasp the significance of that moment, and the challenges that O'Connor would soon face, it's important to remember that back then there was no TikTok, no SoundCloud, not even the internet. Music came into our lives by way of radio and television, filtered through the values, priorities, and machinery of the entertainment industry. Anything that was challenging or subversive was suppressed or shaded, kind of there but not there. Some of us taught ourselves to decode it, like secret messages passed over the transom, stealth blueprints for survival.

When I was six years old, I thought the coolest girl in the world was Leather Tuscadero on *Happy Days*, having no idea that she was played by an even cooler real-life girl, Suzi Quatro (both girls were way cooler than Fonzie). Two years later, Leather Tuscadero was supplanted by the sunglasses-donning, cigarette-smoke-blowing, trash-talking Betty Rizzo. I vividly remember seeing *Grease* in a second-run movie theater with a couple of girls from the neighborhood. They were swooning for Danny, but I was tuning in to another frequency altogether.

When Rizzo started into "There are Worse Things I Could Do" and got to the part where she belts out, "I don't steal and I don't lie, but I can feel and I can cry, a fact I'll bet you never knew, but to cry in front of you, that's the worst thing I could do . . ." I had to bolt for the bathroom stall, where I bawled my eyes out, hurting for the both of us, isolated and alone.

Then, a few years later, Debbie Harry appeared on the *Muppet Show*.[1] I sat mesmerized as she sang a kid-friendly version of "Call Me" with Dr. Teeth and Electric Mayhem as her backing band. "You like her?" my mother inquired accusingly. "Well, she's a junkie and she's gonna drop dead," she said flatly as she walked past the TV set.

What was a junkie? At age eleven I had no idea what that word meant. I'm not even sure my mother did; this was probably a headline she'd seen on the cover of the *National Enquirer*, one of her most trusted news sources. What I saw was that Debbie Harry was beautiful and glamorous, yet somehow familiar, even approachable. When she talked to Kermit and the frog scouts, she moved and sounded just like people I knew.[2] She had the sassy attitude of the person I wanted to become.

After I saw Debbie Harry on the *Muppet Show*, she was suddenly everywhere, her voice coming through the speakers of my dad's car radio, her face on posters in the record store window and the cover of *People* magazine. My older cousin gave me a copy of Blondie's *Autoamerican* for Christmas. Then I worked my way backward through *Eat to the Beat* and *Parallel Lines*.

A couple of years into my Blondie obsession, my mother read *And I Don't Want to Live This Life*, the book Deborah Spungen wrote about her daughter, Nancy, the troubled groupie girlfriend of Sex Pistols bassist Sid Vicious, whose body was found under a bathroom sink at the Chelsea Hotel, rendered lifeless as the result of a heroin overdose or murder. Convinced that I, too, was on the fast track to becoming a dead junkie slut, my mother started combing through my backpack in search of hypodermic needles, which of course I didn't have. She didn't understand that the music was my high, that and some vaguely formed notion that someday I could be a star like Debbie Harry — who, as I write, is still very much alive.[3]

All those years ago I saw something in Debbie Harry that my mother did not and could not see. Still, I had no sense whatsoever of Debbie Harry as an actual living, breathing person. I saw her only as a New Wave rock goddess. How she achieved transcendence was mysterious, yet in my young mind, probably straightforward, too. Step one: write some cool songs. Step two: find a cool band. Step three: play some cool gigs. From there it was just a matter of signing a record deal, releasing an album, and waiting for fame and fortune to follow. You would never have to worry about so much as a zit — no, I was quite sure Debbie Harry never had one. Impossible!

In retrospect, of course, this was ridiculously naive, but I was a kid. What did I know? What did O'Connor know? One minute she's in the backyard shed listening to Bob Dylan records, the next she's learning his songs in reform school, the next she's singing Barbra Streisand songs at her teacher's wedding, and the next after that she's signing her first record deal — while she's still in her teens. It must have seemed like a dream come true. And for a brief moment, it was.

Thanks to her brief stint with In Tua Nua, O'Connor had already made significant connections, including with U2's accountant, Ossie Kilkenny, who introduced her to Bono, who introduced her to Fachtna O'Ceallaigh, then a forty-year-old provocateur known in the industry for his outspoken views on music and politics.[4]

Although he had recently been fired as the head of U2's

Mother Records for complaining that the band (read: Bono) was meddling in the label's affairs, O'Ceallaigh had successfully managed artists including Bananarama and the Boomtown Rats, whom he steered to the top of the UK charts. He was prepared to do the same for his new charge, but she had opinions, which meant she wasn't going to be an "easy" client.

As O'Connor was planning to make her first album for Ensign, U2's the Edge approached her about collaborating on the soundtrack for the 1986 art film *Captive*. Although the movie wasn't a success, music critics took notice of "Heroine," a song that O'Connor and the Edge cowrote and performed with Larry Mullen Jr. Most emerging artists would have been thrilled about the buzz, but not O'Connor, who hated being described as a U2 protégé, and she publicly dismissed the band's music as "bombastic." She was similarly blunt in her assessment of Mick Glossop, the producer Grainge had enlisted to work on her album, disparaging him as a "fucking old hippie."

Glossop had previously worked with punk and New Wave bands such as Magazine and Public Image Ltd. He'd even produced The Waterboys's epic 1985 album *This Is the Sea*. But his most extensive experience was in shaping the softer sounds of Van Morrison, and at Grainge's encouragement, he approached O'Connor's music with the same musical model in mind.

The problem was that this was not at all where O'Connor wanted to go. She protested that Glossop was zapping the life out of her songs and refused to continue working with him. Rather than reining her in, as I'm sure the label would have wanted, O'Ceallaigh encouraged O'Connor to take over the production herself. She did, scrapping the old sessions and starting over almost entirely from scratch.

Even though she was inexperienced, O'Connor was headstrong and determined to prove that she could realize her own creative vision. She surrounded herself with seasoned and skilled collaborators including former Adam and the Ants guitarists Marco Pirroni and Kevin Mooney, former Japan guitarist Rob Dean, former Jah Wobble drummer John Reynolds, former In Tua Nua string player Steve Wickham, and the Irish singing legend Enya. They decamped to a new studio in Camden Town, where they experimented with new arrangements, led by her direction instead of responding to the demands of Grainge and the record company.

Once they hit their stride, recording the album took only a matter of weeks, with O'Connor often laying down her vocals in a single take as U2 engineer Kevin Moloney helmed the console, later mixing the songs along with O'Connor and a few tape operators. In the end, O'Connor's label bosses liked what they heard, but having already blown a hundred thousand pounds on the scrapped recording sessions, they weren't keen on taking any chances on the promo side. They ratcheted up the pressure on O'Connor to release a big hit, something along the lines of U2's 1987 album *The Joshua Tree*, which was on track to become the fastest-selling album in British history . . . or at least for her to put out an album as successful as U2's first efforts, which put them squarely on the map.

The promotional plan was to sell O'Connor on her sex appeal, so they encouraged her to wear her hair long and her skirts short, just like the label heads' mistresses. With her huge, expressive eyes, slender physique, and fair, luminescent skin, O'Connor was unusually beautiful and certainly could have pulled that off, but she wanted to be valued as an artist—not as a sex symbol. At O'Ceallaigh's half-joking suggestion, O'Connor hired a barber to give her a Mohawk, then to shave her head altogether. She ditched her flowery dresses for baggy T-shirts, torn pants, and Doc Martens boots.

These moves might have seemed risky or even reckless, but O'Connor's new look, a combination of vulnerable and tough, matched the person she was becoming. It was also a brand O'Ceallaigh knew that he could sell, but was it an exercise in bad faith? He must have known that O'Connor never wanted to be a star in the mode of pop princesses like Debbie Gibson, Tiffany, or Samantha Fox, nor a sex queen like Madonna, nor a girl-power cartoon like Cyndi Lauper. But did he have a sense of what she really wanted, which was more than just projecting an image?

O'Connor saw herself in the mold of the great Irish artists and agitators, such as the playwright Tom Murphy and the novelist Dermot Bolger. For her, music was a form of DIY primal therapy. She didn't just want to sing. She needed to scream. If other people could hear her, they would see her pain, but also feel her desire for the love and affection she never had as a child. They would relate and respond—and perhaps they could heal, too.

O'Connor's ambition was to become the next Bob Dylan or John Lennon. She saw her debut album as a self-portrait of who she was up to that moment, a collection of stories with tempos, sonic excerpts drawn from her memoir-in-progress. At no point would she come out and directly say the words she would often repeat just a few years later:

My name is Sinéad O'Connor. I am an Irish woman. And I am an abused child. The only reason I ever opened my mouth to sing was so that I could tell my story and have it heard . . . My story is the story of countless millions of children whose families and nations were torn apart in the name of Jesus Christ.[5]

She was even willing to provide alternative explanations of her songs to those who needed to hear them, for example, cheekily claiming that "Drink Before the War" was about an unsupportive school headmaster, "Never Get Old" about a boy she had a crush on. But if you were tuning in, you could pick up on different frequencies, and the truth of these songs was present, even in the radio-friendly singles. "Mandinka" is a rejection of shame. "I Want Your (Hands on Me)" is a reclamation of sexuality. Every other track can be read as an answer song, a reply to O'Connor's mother's vitriol drawing its force from the soft-loud dynamic in her voice, alternating between a grieving whisper and a barely contained rage. Take for example the song "Jerusalem":

Getting tired of you doing this to me
I'm going to hit you if you say that to me
One more time
I want to see you

Or "Just Like U Said It Would B":

When everything's quiet
Will you stay?
Will you be my lover?
Will you be my mama?

Or the album's centerpiece, "Never Get Old," which kicks off with a cameo from Enya reciting Psalm 91:13 in Gaelic, which is roughly translated into English as:

God commanded His angels concerning you
To guard you in all your ways
They will lift you up in their arms
To keep you from striking your foot against a stone
You will tread upon the lion and the cobra
You will trample the great lion and the serpent

O'Connor picks it up from Enya, offering sketches of people searching for solace, her voice soaring ever upward before fading to a close. And that track follows with "Troy" the lament that christened her recording career.

As a whole, O'Connor's album was not so much an act of conscious mythmaking as it was dragon-slaying. Not a typical teenage rejection of the status quo, it was a reflection of her desire to use her voice as a megaphone for expressing what could not otherwise be said or directly acknowledged. Is it any wonder that she called the album *The Lion and the Cobra*? O'Connor expresses regret over being aware of the evils around her and not having the strength to vanquish them, but she also shows that she has the desire to will that strength.

When critics heard her music for the first time, they drew comparisons with other "intense" artists such as Peter Gabriel, Kate Bush, and Siouxsie Sioux. But they missed the remarkable depth of her maturity as a song-writer. O'Connor wrote the songs when she was in her teens, rooted them in her lived experience, and brought all of that energy into the work.

At twenty years old, O'Connor was self-aware enough to know that she was interested in making neither a traditional "Irish" record nor a record that sounded like any other artist who'd come before her. She was confident enough to take the lead and produce her own album, working out how to use digital sampling techniques and idioms from funk, pop, noise, and beyond to make her music come to life in a way that was both eclectic and unified. She wasn't worried about where her record might be filed in retail store bins, or whether she was pretty enough to get it sold.

This doesn't mean O'Connor was completely unwilling to compromise. She provided phony explanations of the songs. She consented to suppressing her Irish accent, following the widely held assumption that this was the only way to sell records in America. She accepted the label's criticism that the image she chose for the album cover, which showed her looking off to the side with her mouth open in song, made her look "too angry" for American audiences. She agreed to sub in another with her mouth shut and her eyes gazing downward.[6]

But on the decisions that mattered most, O'Connor managed to break the rules of the recording industry, and, what's more, she almost got away with it. I say "almost" because O'Connor could see the whole of the moon but never the flame. She was incapable of distinguishing what to bring into the work and what to hold back. For her, experience and expression were all one thing. Above all else, O'Connor wanted to be heard, and she was willing to make sacrifices to do that. That was a strength but also a vulnerability.

As she was working on the album, she became involved

with her drummer, John Reynolds, and got pregnant only a month into their relationship. O'Connor would later say that she put up a calm front, but inside she was terrified. After all she had overcome to get to this point, would the label drop her? Would she have to return to Ireland, to being nothing, and to being deserving of nothing? To being her mother's daughter?

O'Connor says she seriously considered ending the pregnancy, and Ensign executives strongly pressured her to do so, even sending a doctor out to the studio to remind her how much money had been invested in the album, and how much danger she would be putting her baby in if she toured while she was pregnant. But she ultimately refused to accept career and motherhood as an either/or proposition. She scoffed at being told what to do, and she remembered what Sister Margaret told her: God will always be with you. Follow your dreams.

Whether O'Connor's perseverance came from that memory, or the need to prove her mother wrong, what matters most is that O'Connor approached her decision in the same way she approached every decision she had made until that point, taking a "no" and turning it into a "watch me."

Weeks after O'Connor wrapped production on the album, she gave birth to her son, Jake Reynolds. It's his blue and white sleep suit you can see tied around her waist as she performs "Mandinka" at the 1989 Grammys, where she has been nominated for Best Female Rock Vocal Performance.[7] It's just as much a symbol of self-expression as her combat boots, ripped jeans, black bra top, shaved head that was embossed with a Public Enemy logo, and the small gold cross dangling from her ear.

Knowing all of this, I can see that O'Connor isn't just a young singer performing on a stage. I see her shearing apart the false self that was built by her mother's abuse, and trying to sew together her own person, one who cares so much about the truth that she's willing to struggle and sacrifice to get closer to it, damn anyone or anything that tries to get in her way—even when that person is her.

Years ago, in my academic life, I met the artist Jeffrey Schiff when we were both humanities fellows at Wesleyan University. At that time, Schiff had recently premiered an installation—at the Cathedral of Saint John the Divine in New York City—that he called "Potter's Field," the name given to mass burial sites for the unnamed and unclaimed. As an exercise in catharsis, he invited members of the community to leave objects that they wished to renounce inside empty chambers that he had built into a platform at the feet of a statue of the prodigal son, the profligate youth who returns to his father's house to seek forgiveness.[8]

Schiff was amazed by the response—not just by the number of participants but by the range of objects they left behind: jewelry, photographs, letters, a baseball bat, a candy wrapper, even a mouth guard. More surprisingly, some of the objects were stolen by other visitors even though they had little or no monetary value. As artifacts of severed human connections, they still held a powerful charge; the platform became a site for a collective economy based on the circulation of emotion. That got me thinking: What about the kinds of losses that can never be renounced, recapitalized, or recouped? How do we come to terms with them?

When the Grammys were over, O'Connor returned to Ireland and brought Jake's sleep suit to her mother's grave, where she rested it on her tombstone. In her memoir she described this gesture as bringing her mother a "souvenir" from the show, but my gut tells me that it's more like a sacrifice — a memento of loss symbolic of the grandchild she would never meet, the daughter's success she would never share.[9] The image is beautiful, and heartbreaking, and, in a way, representative of who O'Connor was: not fearless or flawless, but wounded and courageous.

This is what comes through in her music, the sense that she is treading close to the lion and the adder, that she knows there is no way to the light except through the darkness. To hear her sing wasn't merely to listen to a collection of pop tunes, or to be entertained by them. It was to witness an intense, if fragile, catharsis that swung between heartbreak and triumph, between destruction and salvation. It was also to experience a bit of that catharsis oneself.

As I write these words, I know that this is a version of the story that no one told in 1987, that no one could tell because the world was not ready to hear it. The idea that O'Connor could be the next Bob Dylan or John Lennon was fundamentally at odds with what the industry and the culture demanded of her or any woman. To show you what I mean, let's go back to 1966, the year of her birth.

AS SEEN ON MTV

In late 1966, Jann Wenner and Ralph Gleason were gearing up to launch *Rolling Stone*, a revolutionary rock-'n'-roll magazine named for two turning points in the formation of the genre: Muddy Waters's 1950 "Rollin' Stone" and Bob Dylan's 1965 "Like A Rolling Stone." When the first issue of the magazine came out in November 1967, John Lennon graced its cover.[1] In the opening pages, Wenner explained that its mission was "not just about the music, but about the things and attitudes that music embraces."[2]

Because it was founded on the lofty premise that rock was a significant social, cultural, and political force, *Rolling Stone* didn't just offer substantive coverage of leading-edge artists and albums. In its pages were boldly told, and often personally informed, stories on such phenomena as Charles Manson, Altamont, and a drug-fueled trip to Las Vegas in search of the American Dream. So committed was the magazine to the counterculture, it offered early subscribers roach clips to hold their joints.[3]

Within the space of just a few years, *Rolling Stone* had proved that it was not only a viable journalistic enterprise but also a kingmaker so powerful that the magazine was name-checked in songs by Joni Mitchell, Pink Floyd, and George Harrison. In 1973, Dr. Hook & the Medicine Show (not to be confused with the Muppets' house band

Dr. Teeth and the Electric Mayhem) even used a parody song about *wanting* to land on the cover of *Rolling Stone* to land on the cover of *Rolling Stone* (drawn as a cartoon caricature).

But in 1977, a decade into its run, Wenner declared San Francisco a "cultural backwater" and moved *Rolling Stone*'s operations to New York, a sign that the self-professed voice of the antiestablishment was comfortable with becoming the establishment. The magazine was no longer able to lay claim to leading or even reflecting the zeitgeist; bands began to sell the covers rather than the other way around. As its core readership aged and rock's glory began to fade, *Rolling Stone* expanded its coverage to include A-list celebrities, entertainment, and pop culture.

Accused of sacrificing substance for style, the magazine started losing subscribers. Advertisers started looking for other ways to reach young, implicitly white, male consumers with money to burn on albums, cars, cigarettes, and booze.

That opportunity came in the form of a new joint venture between American Express and Warner Communications called "Music Television," or MTV for short. When MTV debuted shortly after midnight on August 1, 1981, virtually no one was watching. The fledgling cable TV network wasn't even carried in New York or Los Angeles. But investors saw potential in the explosive growth of cable television, particularly in affluent white suburbs.[4]

Jann Wenner didn't agree. When MTV co-founder Bob Pittman first explained the concept, Wenner told Pittman it would never work.[5] But unlike magazines or radio stations, MTV could reach millions of people at a time twenty-four hours a day, seven days a week.

And the idea of a round-the-clock curated video juke-box wasn't really as out there as it might have appeared. Like album-oriented-rock (AOR) radio, MTV's content was largely determined by music industry executives who leaned on the major labels to provide them with free promotional video clips. These gatekeepers held fast to old assumptions and biases about what audiences wanted to see and hear, so MTV more or less followed the same format as rock radio, whereby the video disc jockeys, also known as veejays, interspersed music videos with peppy banter and music news. The main difference was MTV's vibe, which was self-consciously irreverent and pitched to Gen Xers.

No longer leading with *Rolling Stone*'s starry-eyed idea that music was capable of changing the world, the network premiered an updated "me generation" pitch two years into its run.[6] "I Want My MTV!" kicked off with Mick Jagger shouting the phrase into a camera as a favor to his old friend, MTV executive Les Garland. Pretty soon David Bowie and Pete Townshend were also on board with the savvy promotion, a wink that boiled down to the idea that the audience should want MTV because that's what the artists wanted.

It worked. As cable operators saw the bandwagon rolling into their towns, they signed on to carry the network, which quickly added new subscribers. Before long, MTV was on the air coast to coast, achieving financial viability through ad sales—the same business model used by radio stations and network TV.

For established rock stars, appearing in an "I Want My MTV!" spot wasn't seen as a corporate sellout. It was a badge signifying the artist's membership in an übercool clubhouse, where they could reach younger audiences. The slogan became so popular it landed in Dire Straits's self-referential 1985 song "Money for Nothing," featuring a cameo by Sting, who opens by repeating the phrase in his trademark falsetto.

The song, and its music video, which was among the first to use computer animation, took Dire Straits to the top of the singles chart. *Brothers in Arms* became the first CD to crack a million sales, going on to reach more than thirty million copies worldwide. This was not only a boon for the band but also a significant milestone in establishing the CD as a format and MTV as a conduit for music promotion.

Before long, radio programmers started looking at MTV's playlists to figure out which new artists to put on the air. Record labels became more conscious of rolling out bands not just on how they sounded, but by how they looked. Sure, some of the old macho rockers and their fans grumbled. Dire Straits even poked fun at them in "Money for Nothing," with Mark Knopfler and Sting jokingly singing from that point of view, griping about MTV's elevation of the slick "pretty boys":

See the little faggot with the earring and the make up
Yeah, buddy, that's his own hair
That little faggot got his own jet airplane
That little faggot, he's a millionaire

The casual use of the word "faggot" and the homophobia it reflected played well in an era when virtually no artists were out—not Freddie Mercury, not George Michael. Even Elton John, whose music video for "I'm

Still Standing" featured studded-leather-bikini-clad guys dancing on a French beach, was married to a woman.

Rampant sexism also meant no one had a problem with a song about artists getting "chicks for free." As opposed to the kind you have to pay for? Take a glance at MTV's biggest stars of the '80s: Duran Duran, The Smiths, Tears for Fears, Adam Ant, Echo and the Bunnymen, Devo, ABC, Spandau Ballet, A Flock of Seagulls, and INXS. You'll see that the New Wave was not so much a threat to the old guard as merely an extension of its reach.

From a practical standpoint, bands like Lynyrd Skynyrd and Jethro Tull didn't have enough music videos to fill the airtime. Including younger artists helped MTV to avoid getting stalled in the '70s. Although the New Wavers were rolling in glitzy synthesizers, hairspray, and makeup, the vast majority were still straight, white men—just like the old Boomers who were running the network, just like the presumed younger audience watching at home.

Over on the FM radio dial, programmers faced a similar generational conundrum: exclusively play tunes from aging rockers like the Rolling Stones and Eric Clapton, or be open to including younger bands like The Police and U2? Either way, certain rules were canon law. The morning show must have a cheesy theme song, an arsenal of sound effects, and two guys at the helm, at least one of whom shall have an animal as part of his name: "Mark the Shark" or "Steve the Stallion," for example. Thou shalt play the all-request rock blocks at lunchtime, and "get the Led out" during the drive at five. Thou shalt not play two women in a row. There can only be one Janis . . . and one Jimi.

Even though Black artists were the architects of rock-'n'-roll, they were virtually nowhere to be found on rock radio. The rewriting—and whitewashing—of the genre's origins is captured in the 1985 blockbuster *Back to the Future*, where a white teenage boy, Marty McFly, goes back to 1955 to invent rock-'n'-roll so that his parents can fall in love and his existence is ensured. This feat is engineered at a dance where Marty takes the stage and rips into "Johnny B. Goode" with a Black backing band struggling to keep up.[7] Once they hit their stride, one of Marty's bandmates rushes offstage to call an offscreen Chuck Berry. "It's me, your cousin, Marvin Berry," he shouts into the phone. "You know that new sound you've been looking for? Well, listen to this!"

The scene was played for laughs—after all, everyone knows that Chuck Berry wrote "Johnny B. Goode." But did you know that the song was partially autobiographical, and that Berry changed the lyrics from "colored boy" to "country boy" in the hopes of getting it played on the radio?[8] Did you know that while Marty McFly was inventing rock in a fictional 1955, the white man who coined the term "rock-'n'-roll" was playing Berry's "Maybellene" at WINS in New York for two hours straight, and sending it to the top of the pop charts?[9]

Among the first disc jockeys of the era to play original songs by Black artists rather than white cover versions, Alan Freed proved that the genre had cross-racial appeal. But before you hail him as a hero, note that, as Berry later discovered, Freed also took the liberty of falsely crediting himself as one of the songwriters, which entitled him to royalties. This was a common practice in the payola era.

Meanwhile, down south, Elvis Presley started adding "Maybellene" to his sets, along with several other songs that were written by Black men whose contributions have never been fully recognized, nor fairly compensated. Arthur Crudup wrote Presley's first single, "That's All Right" (often called the first rock-'n'-roll song) and several more, including "My Baby Left Me." Otis Blackwell wrote other Presley hits, such as "All Shook Up," "Don't Be Cruel," and "Return to Sender," plus more than a thousand other songs, including "Great Balls of Fire," "Fever," and "Breathless," that became career- and genre-defining hits for white artists, including Jerry Lee Lewis and Peggy Lee.

This history was—and still is—largely unknown to most white people. So is the fact that three decades later the music industry was still viewing race as the determining factor in who got to make music in particular genres, and to whom that music would be promoted.

R&B was targeted to Black kids, rock-'n'-roll to whites. "Crossover" was industry code for Black artists who could build up their appeal in R&B and then cross over the color line into pop and rock, where the presumed record buyers were. Labels considered these artists an exceedingly rare commodity. Therefore, better to push Pat Boone's version of "Ain't That a Shame" than Fats Domino's on pop and rock stations, Led Zeppelin's "Whole Lotta Love" instead of Willie Dixon/Muddy Waters's "You Need Love," Eric Clapton's soft rock cover of "I Shot the Sheriff" rather than Bob Marley and the Wailers's original reggae protest song.

You may point out that by 1985—the same year that "Money for Nothing" and *Back to the Future* were released—things had changed. After all, Tina Turner won four of the six Grammys for which her 1984 album *Private Dancer* had been nominated, and she embarked on a hugely successful 180-date international tour that positioned her as one of the biggest stars of the pop world. You would be right to note that *Private Dancer* was certified 5× platinum in the United States and sold more than twelve million copies worldwide. Certainly, these accomplishments show that Turner was able to successfully appeal to a broad range of audiences, and to boot she did so at age forty-five, not as a young starlet who'd been hatched by marketing gurus for the video age.[10]

But when Turner signed with Capitol a year before releasing *Private Dancer*, she was discounted as an R&B has-been. In the 2021 documentary *TINA*, we learn that A&R rep John Carter was ridiculed by a label executive who incredulously asked, "Carter, you signed this old [N-word] douchebag?" After the label nearly dropped Turner, Capitol gave her a modest budget and only two weeks to record *Private Dancer*, the album that would reset her career and prove that audiences were far ahead of the industry in how they saw race.[11]

Outrageously, it took until 2019 for *Private Dancer* to be preserved by the National Recording Registry at the Library of Congress, recognized for being "culturally, historically, or aesthetically significant."[12] The Rock & Roll Hall of Fame called Turner the undisputed "Queen of Rock," who "worked hard to reimagine the role of a Black woman in rock and roll—one not relegated to the edges," but did not induct her as a solo performer until 2021.[13] (Ike and Tina Turner, on the other hand, were inducted in 1991 by Phil Spector.)

To succeed in 1985, Turner had to be "exceptional" in both senses of the word. She was exceptional in terms of her talent and drive, the qualities that helped her overcome the music industry's pervasive racism, sexism, and ageism.

She was also exceptional in the sense of being an exception to the rule. She was certainly not proof that there was no rule, no musical apartheid.[14]

Perhaps describing the music industry's segregationist policies as "apartheid" seems overly dramatic. After all, 1985 was the same year that Little Steven Van Zandt and the producer Arthur Baker formed the protest group Artists United Against Apartheid, which released a song called "Sun City" in order to expose and bring an end to South Africa's abhorrent systemic apartheid.[15] Van Zandt and Baker's effort, which brought together Black and white artists singing about how they refused to perform at the South African Sun City casino and resort, went on to raise public awareness and more than a million dollars to fight apartheid.

But far less often discussed is that at the time of the song's release, only half of US radio stations agreed to play "Sun City." Citing its "political" content, PBS refused to broadcast a documentary about the making of the song, and artists such as the Beach Boys, Rod Stewart, Elton John, and Queen continued to perform there. In recent years Van Zandt has also been candid about how industry power players balked at the participation of rappers in the release of "Sun City" even though the song's opening lines were "We're rockers and rappers united and strong / We're here to talk about South Africa / We don't like what's going on."[16]

How much of this was known to O'Connor? Likely very little. She was eighteen when she signed her contract with Ensign in 1985. Her romantic ideas about the music industry's self-professed countercultural values and progressive priorities were likely informed by the mythos of a magazine that once pointed to Muddy Waters, Bob Dylan, and John Lennon as its holy trinity, and by its Irish analogue, *Hot Press*. Even today, the latter publication claims on its website that it has "rattled the cages of Irish society" since its 1977 inception. If only that were true.

ROCK-'N'-ROLL CASSANDRA

"Black music" simply did not fit in with the rock format that MTV was modeled on — or at least that was the excuse that the network always floated to justify its exclusionary policies, and the line veejay Mark Goodman gave to David Bowie when Bowie famously challenged Goodman on air in 1983.[1] It's also the line many white viewers of MTV believed because we'd come up listening to radio stations that were similarly segregated. This began to change *very slowly* thanks in large part to the talents and accomplishments of a single artist.[2]

Michael Jackson rose to fame as a child sensation and the most prominent member of the Jackson 5, which in 1970 was the first group to score four consecutive number-one pop hits.[3] Nine years later, Jackson teamed up with producer Quincy Jones for *Off the Wall*, his fifth solo studio album and first for Epic Records.

In 1979, the music industry was still deeply segregated, but Jackson's lead single, "Don't Stop 'Til You Get Enough," was promoted to R&B and pop formats at the same time, which helped the song reach the top of the charts in nine countries. Even so, Jackson continued to encounter resistance from the white rock establishment. Breaking through that barrier wasn't simply a matter of personal ambition, or global ascension, but a push for equality of opportunity.

In response to *Rolling Stone*'s decision to deny him a spot on its cover, Jackson was widely quoted as saying, "I've been told over and over that black people on the cover of magazines doesn't sell copies . . . Just wait. Someday those magazines are going to be begging me for an interview. Maybe I'll give them one, and maybe I won't."[4]

Jackson pushed ahead, pursuing a collaboration with Freddie Mercury of Queen, sometime around 1981. Mercury was reportedly unhappy that Jackson brought a llama into the recording studio, and Jackson disliked Mercury's prolific drug use.[5] Their plans to release an album together were scrapped, but Jackson kept going.

He and Quincy Jones worked their way through more than seven hundred demos for his next solo studio album, *Thriller*. They consciously brought in a mix of musical genres, looking to transcend radio format boundaries and reach the broadest possible audience. When they got to "Beat It," Jones encouraged Jackson to work with a rock icon.[6] After Pete Townshend turned down the request, Jackson tapped Eddie Van Halen, who agreed to play guitar on the track and ended up assisting Jackson on the arrangement. Whether or not Van Halen's blistering solos set a monitor speaker on fire during the recording sessions, as legend has it, his contributions did stamp "Beat It" as legit for rock stations.[7]

It's notable that Van Halen wasn't paid for his work, nor did he initially take credit for it. He's said to have asked for only a case of beer and a dance lesson from Jackson as compensation. This has often been described as an expression of his modesty, or, more practically, his desire not to violate the terms of his band's noncompete agreement. But it's at least as likely that he was reluctant to be seen as crossing the line into R&B.[8]

Van Halen could not have known then that after its November 1982 release, *Thriller* would go on to be the first major label album to debut worldwide, the first to be marketed to multiple radio formats simultaneously, and the first to be worked for a marathon stretch of two years, with seven songs being pushed as singles rather than the usual two or three.

But to become the King of Pop, Jackson needed to overcome one more obstacle. MTV had reservations about playing his videos, expressing skepticism that any Black artist would appeal to its target majority white twelve- to thirty-four-year-old demographic.[9] Although MTV's VP of programming, Les Garland, would later claim that the network had always embraced Jackson, others, such as CBS label president Walter Yetnikoff, have disputed that characterization, pointing out that its decision to play the video for *Thriller*'s first single, "Billie Jean," came about only after the label threatened to pull its white artists from the network.[10]

Whichever account you believe, it's indisputable that "Billie Jean" was already a massive radio hit when MTV started playing the video, and Jackson was the first Black artist in MTV's history to have videos played in heavy rotation. It's also indisputable that those videos had a major effect on popular culture.

"Billie Jean" inspired kids across the country to imitate Jackson's look, replete with untied shoes, studded belts, and single white gloves. "Beat It" introduced the world to an entirely new genre—the syncopated dance routine.

The million-dollar extended video for the album's title track, "Thriller," set a new standard for music videos, and it took MTV's audience from around 1.2 million into the tens of millions.[11]

As Jackson's star rose, *Thriller* edged out Men at Work's *Business as Usual* for the top spot on the Billboard 200 album chart, where it would remain for thirty-seven non-consecutive weeks, from February 1983 to April 1984. Its sales outpaced heavily promoted rock albums, including Van Halen's *1984*. *Thriller* went on to become the best-selling album of all time. Certified 34× platinum by the Recording Industry of America (RIAA) in 2021, it has sold more than 70 million copies worldwide.[12]

MTV wasn't only good for Jackson, Jackson was good for MTV. While there is no doubt that Jackson's success opened doors for other Black artists, such as Run-DMC and Living Colour, it's important not to overlook the significant racism that remained prevalent through the '80s and beyond.

When Don Letts directed the 1982 video for Musical Youth's "Pass the Dutchie," one of the first videos shown on MTV to feature Black artists, he filmed on the southern banks of the Thames River, centering neighborhoods where Black culture flourished. But Letts also put a lot of white extras in the video, which meant that his statement might have slipped under the radar. He was invited to MTV's studios to be interviewed on air about directing videos for the Clash, but executives didn't realize he was Black. When Letts showed up, they told him they would have to abort the segment.[13]

When Run-DMC and Aerosmith collaborated on a reimagined version of "Walk this Way" in 1986, it became the first rap song to crack the Billboard Top 10. But it was white producer Rick Rubin whom the *Village Voice* crowned "King of Rap" for dusting off Aerosmith's 1975 hit and masterminding the redo as a comeback for a rock band that had been out of the spotlight for years.[14] The music video, which saw heavy rotation on MTV, shows white rocker Steven Tyler literally knocking down the wall between rap and rock, as though the whole thing had been his idea.

In 1986, MTV was also all about the Beastie Boys, whose debut *Licensed to Ill* was originally going to be called *Don't Be a Faggot*. In addition to extolling the virtues of sniffing glue and smoking Angel dust and crack, the all-white Beasties rapped about penetrating a girl with a whiffle bat and the virtues of Spanish flies. The band's stage show featured a half-naked dancer in a cage and a giant hydraulic penis.[15] Although the band soon reformed and Adam Horovitz later publicly apologized for this and much of its "bad boy" behavior in its beer-swilling hard-partying days, MTV had no problem with the early Beasties fighting for their right to party — or pussy — as the concertgoers shouted.

Fighting the power was another matter entirely. While *Licensed to Ill* became the first rap record to top the Billboard 200 chart, MTV refused to play music videos from Black rap artists like Public Enemy and N.W.A.[16] It also continued to reject videos for R&B artists, even saying no to the video for the lead single from Whitney Houston's 1985 self-titled debut, "You Give Good Love."

"What were your earliest memories of MTV?" an off-camera reporter once asked Houston in an interview for *MTV News* in 2001. "That I couldn't get on," she replied, going on to candidly discuss the discrimination she experienced. Houston said she was told it was only for rock artists, meaning white artists. "Jimi Hendrix is dead," she said, explaining that Black artists had to both fit and break the format to get on.

It was only after another single, "Saving All My Love for You," became a huge crossover hit on radio that MTV's programmers reconsidered. Houston explained they had no choice but to play it: "I love it when they have no choice," she said smiling, "I love it, I love it." It wasn't until her third hit single, "How Will I Know," that MTV really got behind her.[7]

MTV was more receptive to white female artists, but the lane was not nearly as open as it may have seemed. Airplay of Madonna's disco-pop tunes "Holiday," "Borderline," and "Lucky Star" rocketed her 1983 self-titled debut album to the top of the pop charts in multiple countries. When Madonna performed "Like a Virgin" at the first-ever MTV Video Music Awards in 1984, it was as momentous a pop culture moment as Elvis shaking his hips on *Ed Sullivan*. But no one saw this as the beginning of a new era where female artists would command promotion or respect equal to that of their male counterparts.

In fact, when Sire Records quietly released Madonna's first single, "Everybody," in 1982, there weren't any music videos or photos of the artist, only a record sleeve with a generic collage of urban street images. Like the recording industry as a whole, Sire executives thought that the only white audiences who would embrace it would be gay men, and Black audiences would only buy it if they believed Madonna was Black.

To prove that she could sell "Everybody" to everybody, Madonna took matters into her own hands, inviting label executives to see her perform the song at New York City's

Danceteria along with a multiracial dance troupe. She also enlisted friends to pack the club that night, impressing executives enough to convince them to cough up $1,500 for her to hire a director to film a scrappy re-creation of the performance. Madonna sent that video to dance clubs around the country, then visited many of those clubs herself, building up her fanbase one dance floor at a time.[18]

Though effective, Madonna's strategy didn't exactly scale. She didn't break the industry's rules so much as she appeared to have mastered them, largely by exploiting her own sexuality. In contrast, Cyndi Lauper, who came up through New York's club scene at the same time as Madonna and broke on MTV the same year with her 1983 debut *She's So Unusual*, was marketed as her inverse, desexualized as a cartoony pop-friendly punk who hung out with pro wrestlers and a dog named Sparkle.[19]

Most women on MTV weren't artists at all, but rather barely clothed extras in videos by hair metal bands, exemplified by future reality TV star Tawny Kitaen, who "acted" for hair metal gods Ratt and Whitesnake and dated members of the latter band.[20] No matter; by the late '80s, MTV was in more than forty-eight million American homes, essentially serving as twenty-four-hour advertising for the record labels.[21] The network was also shown on TVs in record stores, and new albums came with stickers declaring "as seen on MTV." You can see how MTV might have seemed like the perfect promotional vehicle to break an emerging artist like Sinéad O'Connor, whose looks were as striking as her voice.[22]

To promote her debut album, *The Lion and the Cobra*, O'Connor had tried the traditional route, traveling across Europe and sitting for upwards of ten traditional press interviews a day, while also caring for her son, Jake, who was only a few months old. She was exhausted and painfully self-conscious, and, unlike Madonna, terrible at self-promotion.

But she was excellent at expressing herself through her music, an asset not lost on John Maybury, an edgy young director who got his start working with the experimental filmmaker Derek Jarman. Whereas the first music videos were low-budget affairs, they had since become high-concept films with sophisticated plots and storylines, something Maybury could work with.

When he met up with O'Connor in Dublin to direct the music video for her lead single, "Troy," Maybury recognized that her look was central to her brand. Rather than concealing it, he suggested that she shave her buzzcut hair completely, then filmed her set against a pitch-black background, and then again in an open field that was deeply saturated in black and white.

In one shot, O'Connor's shoulders are bare. In another, white lights flicker against her skin. Then gold rain pours down on her. She spins around in a circle until it covers her. Then she sings inside a circle of fire, and at the end, she emerges triumphantly, wearing a white gown. Maybury's daring visual effort paid off; after the song became a video hit in the Netherlands, it set the stage for O'Connor's introduction in the United States.

Maybury went on to direct O'Connor's next video, for "Mandinka," which was also shot in extreme close-up. Echoing the song's message about a woman's refusal to accept the status quo, O'Connor this time wears an oversized leather jacket, strums a guitar, and strikes a powerful pose.

After premiering on MTV's *120 Minutes* in January 1988, the video went into heavy rotation, propelling her single to the top of the dance chart. Her next single, "I Want Your Hands (on Me)," also enjoyed significant MTV promotion, signaling the arrival of a new kind of female pop star — not an overt sex symbol like Madonna or an eccentric like Cyndi Lauper — but someone who was sexy in her eccentricity, and unapologetically original.[23]

Being Irish certainly helped too. U2 was already world famous. Enya was about to break with her massive international hit "Orinoco Flow," also known as "Sail Away." As white audiences became fascinated by these vaguely exotic artists, O'Connor's music landed on soundtracks for *Nightmare on Elm Street IV* and *Miami Vice*, and she was invited to perform on *Late Night with David Letterman*.

Up until this point, O'Connor hadn't done very many interviews in the United States. Outside of her music and music videos, people didn't really have a sense of who she was or what to make of her. She probably would have preferred that it remain that way. Whenever she sat down with reporters, who dug around for insight from her earliest European press coverage, O'Connor came across as demure, reticent, once speaking so quietly a reporter asked her to speak into a cassette recorder so he could transcribe her responses later on.

She was constantly questioned about why she appeared "intense" in her music videos, why she always seemed to have a "rage burning inside." O'Connor rarely pushed back against these characterizations or owned them. She just smiled and shrugged them off, or made winking, self-deprecating jokes about them. Whenever she was asked about "sizzling" details from her past, such as her history of shoplifting and working as a kiss-o-gram girl, she made light of them, giggling along with the interviewers, who seemed both fascinated and puzzled by this mysterious waiflike, almost alien, creature.[24]

Reporters invariably asked O'Connor about her hairstyle, which she didn't get into, except to acknowledge that it was potentially intimidating until people realized that she was actually really nice and sweet. On the rare occasions when she was asked about her music, she smiled and shyly said, "I don't know," as if to show how nice and sweet she really was.

The predicament O'Connor faced was not only being a twenty-year-old trying to navigate sudden and overwhelming fame but also doing so as a young woman whose ambitions were far more in line with the fantasy of being a protest singer than the reality of being pushed as a pop star. While it was totally cool for U2, Michael Stipe, and Sting to flaunt their activist bona fides, female artists were supposed to stick to the music, singing sexual come-ons, love songs, or songs about nothing, baby, baby, baby.

O'Connor's touchstones were not pop stars, or stadium rockers. Aside from her childhood Christian-era Dylan obsession and her love for the Beatles (especially John Lennon), her tastes largely coalesced around music that wasn't being played on any video network or radio station — namely, the reggae records that Fachtna O'Ceallaigh introduced her to in London.

O'Ceallaigh bought everything on the Jamaican charts, his record collection filling an entire room of his flat. He played O'Connor songs by artists like Barrington Levy and Prince Buster, and introduced her to personal contacts, including his friend who ran a pirate radio station called the Dread Broadcasting Corporation and a stall on Portobello Road where he sold reggae records.

O'Connor fell in love with the stories in these songs, the emotions in the singing, and maybe most of all the way reggae drew people in. She watched with awe as O'Ceallaigh's friend set up a mic in front of his record stall and played "riddim" versions of the hits—backing tracks without vocals. Passersby took shots at their own version of karaoke, making up their own lyrics and melodies on the spot, approaching these impromptu performances passionately and competitively.

Although she couldn't easily understand their accents, O'Connor managed to make out a few words, such as "burn," "pope," "Babylon," and "blood," that would become central to her own musical vocabulary. As she realized that reggae was more than a musical style, she desperately tried to connect with older Rasta men. She listened intently as they talked about Ireland and its colonization—not football or politics. To her, they spoke like priests, yet their version of Scripture was revolutionary, modeling for O'Connor an idealized, spiritualized, and perhaps even fetishized concept of Black masculinity.

O'Connor saw these men as benevolent and protective, calling them "watchers" akin to "God's security detail." Her complicated admiration soon morphed into an even more complicated identification with Blackness based heavily on her own experiences of oppression—and a deep desire to disidentify with racist oppressors.

She would soon tell reporters that her first hit, "Mandinka," was inspired by watching the American TV series *Roots* as a child and how she "came to emotionally identify with the civil rights movement and slavery, especially given the theocracy I lived in and the oppression of my own home."[25] In 1991, she went even further, telling *Esquire*, "I feel I have much more in common with black people culturally, maybe because I'm Irish and it's a similar culture."[26]

Back then O'Connor didn't have the framework or language to grasp, much less articulate, the difference between her experiences and theirs. The culture didn't either.[27] Though we may now clearly see the problematic nature of these false equivalencies, we can also clearly see that O'Connor's intentions were antiracist. She proceeded to consistently denounce racism, stand in solidarity with Black artists, and record her own reggae songs, often in collaboration with Black reggae legends, such as Sly and Robbie. But first she had to make it past the gatekeepers and the censors, and that was not easy in the context of deep systemic racism.

By the close of 1988 *The Lion and the Cobra* had vaulted to the number 36 spot on the US Billboard 200 chart, and O'Connor ended up selling in excess of 500,000 copies of the album when the label had predicted that she'd only achieve a quarter of that number. It was that enormous commercial success, and not necessarily the big messages in her songs, that led to O'Connor earning her first Grammy nomination—for "Best Female Rock Vocal Performance."

For most emerging artists, this would have been an incredible cause for celebration. But there was a problem. The 1989 Grammys were swirling in a long-in-the-making controversy. The powerful white men who controlled the industry considered rap either a passing fad or dangerously subversive. Yet rap had become too popular to simply ignore. Even MTV had come around to that reality, premiering *Yo! MTV Raps*, first in Europe in 1987 and then in the US in 1988.

The Recording Academy announced that it would present the first-ever Grammy award for "Best Rap Performance," but, citing limited airtime, the presentation would not be televised. In response, several nominees boycotted the ceremony, including DJ Jazzy Jeff & the Fresh Prince, who would ultimately win for their G-rated hit "Parents Just Don't Understand."

O'Connor was deeply opposed to the Academy's stance. On her first US tour she made it a point of seeking out local rap artists to open her dates.[28] She was also a passionate fan of the bands that the industry wanted most to suppress, like N.W.A. and Public Enemy, whose music took on racism and the media, politics, and class struggle.

Before it was common for white artists to take a public stand against racism in the United States, O'Connor identified with and shared the desire of rappers to make music with meaning. She understood that the decision not to consider these artists as nominees, and not to televise the presentation of the "Best Rap Performance" award, amounted to racial discrimination and political repression.

At the same time, she was scheduled to perform "Mandinka," at the ceremony. Her late-night appearance on *Letterman* aside, this would be her first exposure on primetime US network TV. There would be tens of millions of people watching, a chance for her to make her mark without any of the awkwardness she experienced in her interviews, without having to slog through dumb questions about her haircut or her days as a kiss-o-gram girl.

Had she been careerist, O'Connor could have played

it safe that night, lip-syncing her way through her song and ending with a gracious smile and a bow. Instead, she used her appearance to call attention to inequities in the industry. As a fuck-you to the label heads, O'Connor wore her son Jake's sleep suit tied behind her waist—a subtle gesture that audiences might have missed. But they could not miss that she performed with an enormous gold Public Enemy logo shaved into the side of her close-cropped hair, a symbol of her solidarity with rap artists who had been erased from the program.

O'Connor lost "Best Female Rock Vocal Performance" to Tina Turner, though she became the talk of the evening, telegraphing the fierceness she had held back in her interviews but that was always present in her music. It was a crucial turning point—not just in terms of her visibility but also in terms of the way that she was seen by others.

Looking back at the late 1987 release of *The Lion and the Cobra*, this turn of events was clearly foreshadowed. *Rolling Stone*'s Anthony DeCurtis gave the album a rave review, crediting O'Connor with "shattering the boundaries of pop music."[29] The *New York Times*'s Jon Pareles lauded her for "[defying] rock's usual roles for women, including flirt, sensitive soul, tough gal, and one of the boys, by claiming and transforming them."[30]

But Pareles also saw something else in O'Connor's music: the threat she represented to the industry and society. He was the first to anticipate the coming backlash, predicting that she may well go on to become a "rock-'n'-roll Cassandra."

*SPIN*NING SINÉAD

It turned out that Jon Pareles was right, but MTV alone was not to blame. As younger music fans flocked to the network, they expressed a hunger for music media that reflected the changing landscape. Bob Guccione Jr. founded *SPIN* magazine in 1985 with the express ambition of serving that role.

Like its predecessor *Rolling Stone*, *SPIN* set out to prove that "alternative" wasn't just a musical genre, but a lifestyle, a worldview, and, of course, a lucrative market. To signal that he wasn't simply a spin-off of his porn-peddling father, *Penthouse* founder Bob Guccione, the younger Guccione put Madonna on *SPIN*'s first cover, a decision that was great for hype but entailed little risk, given that Madonna was already one of the biggest pop stars in the world.

SPIN went on to treat "intense" white male artists, such as Bono, Noel Gallagher, and Kurt Cobain, with deep reverence.[1] It was superficially receptive to male rap and hip-hop artists, although interviews with Ice Cube and LL Cool J show that its racial politics were deeply conflicted.[2] With women, not so much.

Two months into its run, *SPIN* put Annie Lennox on its August 1985 cover but also ran a profile entitled "What Ike Had to Do With It: The Flipside to Tina's Story." In the piece, reporter Ed Kiersh fails to challenge Ike Turner's self-serving justifications for spousal abuse and instead reminds readers of his musical genius. This isn't merely my interpretation, but that of Guccione Jr. himself.

As part of a thirtieth-anniversary celebration of *SPIN*, which was posted on the *Daily Beast* in 2015, Kiersh's story was reprinted along with an editor's note in which Guccione Jr. recounted planning it in response to Tina Turner's whirlwind comeback. Guccione Jr. praised Ike Turner for "inventing rock-'n'-roll." At the same time, he said of Tina's abuse, "She frankly milked that a bit when she was caught up on a tide of universal sympathy."[3]

Showing a similar attitude, before the Red Hot Chili Peppers broke big in 1991, *SPIN* had no problem putting the band on its February 1990 cover, hyping them even though front man Anthony Kiedis had recently been arrested for sexual battery after a show in Virginia, an incident recounted in the story as a brag.[4] Reporter Dean Kuipers opens with a late-1989 show in Green Bay, Wisconsin, which he describes as a glorious bacchanalian free-for-all, where the band's socks on cocks routine "made virgins cry."[5]

Unsurprisingly, *SPIN* and Guccione Jr. himself were sued by a female staffer for sexual harassment and gender discrimination in 1994.[6] During the trial, witnesses testified that in addition to experiencing pay disparities and limited opportunities for advancement, women were routinely subjected to sexist comments, unwanted touching, and sexual propositioning. They said Guccione Jr.'s reputation for flirting with and dating young female employees was only the tip of the iceberg—they were even asked to edit stories naked.[7]

Among those to take the stand was Lauren Spencer, then a writer and senior editor, who later recounted the proceedings in a first-person essay appearing in *Jane*.[8] On the one hand, Spencer said, she got to cover the exploding grunge scene, forming friendships she describes as "validating the dreams that had lured her into the rock-'n'-roll industry." On the other hand, she was asked by Guccione Jr. whether she'd "gotten lucky" with her interview subjects and was routinely told that "girls can't write." Spencer recalled being called "a stupid cunt," and relayed that the magazine's female general manager said she was not comfortable raising harassment issues with Guccione Jr. for fear of not being taken seriously.[9]

Given this toxic environment, is it any wonder that *SPIN* would have problems with an artist like O'Connor? Over the course of her career, Guccione Jr. would repeatedly claim that he "discovered" her, taking credit for O'Connor's success while consistently undermining it. The pattern began with Guccione Jr.'s questionable assertion that he found a promotional cassette tape of *The Lion and the Cobra* in a trash can at *SPIN* in late 1987, and then phoned O'Connor's publicist, Elaine Shock, for an interview, only to be told that he was the only American journalist to express interest.[10] For her part, Shock says she remembers the exchange differently.[11]

Guccione Jr. has also called his decision to include O'Connor in *SPIN*'s 1988 "Top 10 Artists to Watch" list "prophetic," ignoring the fact that she had already been covered by major US media outlets, including *Rolling Stone* and the *New York Times*, and featured extensively on MTV. In fact, *SPIN*'s first coverage of O'Connor was a scant single column spread in January 1988 credited to Elin

Wilder. It is paired with a large topless photo by Anton Corbijn where O'Connor's arms are provocatively placed across her chest.[12]

Notably, a full-page ad for *The Lion and the Cobra* appears in the same issue of the magazine, revealing the razor-thin line between *SPIN*'s "journalism" and its sponsored content. Although *SPIN* went on to include O'Connor's debut in the number twenty-four spot on its twenty-five "Greatest Albums of All Time" list, that hype came in April 1989, a full year after *The Lion and the Cobra* had peaked at number thirty-six on the Billboard 200 chart.[13]

O'Connor doesn't substantively appear in *SPIN* again until its April 1990 issue, a full year later. By then *The Lion and the Cobra* had been certified gold, and the lead single from her second album, *I Do Not Want What I Haven't Got*, "Nothing Compares 2 U," was a platinum-selling megahit in the United States as well as Europe and Australia.[14]

Rather than leading with these accomplishments, Legs McNeil, who was one of the alleged perpetrators named in the sexual harassment lawsuit, opens with this teaser: "For 21 years, she fought to do it her way. But when she won and her dream came true, the torment continued."[15] He goes on to suggest that O'Connor was an artist who got to the top not by any legitimate means, but by manipulating her fans.

Without any support except fleeting references to her troubled personal history, McNeil claimed that O'Connor was tormented by the myth that she had created, that "the persona she unleashed was a study in contradiction— the ultimate victim-savior, child-woman, Madonna and whore, rock star and school girl."

McNeil then reaches back to meeting O'Connor for the

first time in the London offices of Chrysalis Records in November 1988 as a setup for his recollection that "Sinéad was the sexiest woman I'd met in a long while. Dazzling and captivating eyes, the most beautiful Irish brogue and skin that looks like it would melt butter. I wanted to stare at her but I was trying to be cool, you know, just catching a glimpse of her when she wasn't looking my way."

No interview came out of their professional meeting, if it even occurred, no feature story, no review. Instead, McNeil fast-forwards to a few months later, when he recalls meeting her again, after she calls him to tell him that she's coming to New York. McNeil says he's bummed because he's having a reading that night, and there will be other women there. McNeil expresses worry about how they are going to deal with O'Connor, and how she will deal with them.

Better than imagined, he says. "By keeping the focus on me, we didn't have to concentrate on what was going on with her. The fact was that after all the success and acclaim Sinéad was experiencing, she was still a desperately unhappy little girl."

McNeil then describes O'Connor returning to his place the next day, where he educates her about music by making her listen to the New York Dolls and Richard Hell, while lamenting her preference for rap. They take a cab ride together, and he flirts with her, confiding to the readers that he's annoyed at the driver for crotch-blocking him.

Have you ever seen a profile of a male artist by a rock journalist that involved ignoring their music completely while infantilizing them, commenting extensively on their manipulative personality and seductive appearance, and expressing concern that inviting the artist to hang out with their exes is going to incite jealousy? Name one where the profile ends with the journalist imposing his musical tastes on the artist, then taking him on a flirtatious taxi ride, and then complaining about the journalist's failure to get laid.

My point isn't to single out McNeil, but rather to show that he wasn't a random hack, and *SPIN* wasn't an obscure entertainment rag. On the contrary, in the early '90s, McNeil was considered a leading voice of the rock establishment, who rose to prominence as a cofounder and "resident punk" of the short-lived but highly influential *PUNK* magazine two decades earlier. During McNeil's tenure at *SPIN*, the magazine had hundreds of thousands of readers. It played a significant role not only in the growth of "alternative rock" but also in what it was and could be as a musical genre and a cultural voice.

Unfortunately, *SPIN*'s approach to writing about female artists was much more the rule than the exception across the music press of that time, even on rare occasions when the reporter was a woman.[16] And how could it not be? Although *SPIN* may have been egregious, female music reporters were invariably working at publications made by men and for men; their ability to get ahead was predicated on playing along, being one of the boys, and/or taking down other women to hoist themselves up.

A striking but not unusual example of how this played out is Sheila Rogers's October 1990 profile for *Rolling Stone*, which she opened by describing O'Connor's Toronto show as "mesmerizing" but then immediately pivoted to a dissection of her postconcert rituals, telling readers that after the show O'Connor was blasting rap music from her boombox "like a child clutching a favorite toy."[17]

I realize as I'm telling you all of this that you may have

never watched MTV music videos or read *SPIN* or *Rolling Stone*. Or you did, but you haven't thought about this stuff for a while. If so, call up a video of O'Connor from YouTube or a track from Spotify and listen to one of her live performances of "Nothing Compares 2 U" from that era.

When do you start crying? Do you even get to the part where she begins to sustain a single note, a deep howl of anguish, building into a gust? Or is it when she begins to whisper the line about the dead flowers? When the song is over, ask yourself why the music journalists, through whom our perceptions and tastes were filtered, needed to infantilize O'Connor, to sexualize and disarm her rather than taking her seriously as an artist.

SHE'LL TALK BUT YOU WON'T LISTEN

In the buzzy months between O'Connor's 1989 Grammy performance and the 1990 release of *I Do Not Want What I Haven't Got*, it isn't hard to imagine what Nigel Grainge and his label partners were thinking: *Shouldn't O'Connor be taking it to the next level, playing into the "victim-savior, child-woman, Madonna and whore, rock star and school girl" role that McNeil and others cooked up? She's so beautiful. And talented! Why does she have to kick the album off with a recitation of the Serenity Prayer? Why does she need to keep singing about her dead mother? Her miscarriages? Does she have to slap a seventeenth-century Irish poem on top of James Brown's "Funky Drummer"? Would it kill her to write a simple pop song, for Chrissake?*

Grainge knew *I Do Not Want What I Haven't Got* would be coming out the same year as Janet Jackson's *Rhythm Nation*, Michael Bolton's *Soul Provider*, and Aerosmith's *Pump*. He considered O'Connor's new slate of songs too personal, too dark, and too intense. He sternly warned her that the release would turn out like Terence Trent D'Arby's sophomore effort, collecting dust in a warehouse, marking the beginning of the end of her brief career.[1]

Not that O'Connor cared what Grainge thought. She still wanted to be a political troubadour, her definition of an artist. Consequently, "Black Boys on Mopeds" addresses the deadly consequences of racism, its lyrics referencing the 1989 death of a young Black man, Nicholas Bramble, who lost his life in a road crash on his scooter after being chased by police, who wrongly assumed he had stolen the vehicle. She dedicated the song—and the entire album—to the family of twenty-one-year-old Colin Roach, another Black man who died in police custody. A photo of Roach's grieving parents standing in front of his image appears in the liner notes with the inscription "God's place is the world; but the world is not God's place."

She makes her views of the music industry plain as day on "The Emperor's New Clothes," in which she disses the Grainges of the world: "And there's millions of people / To offer advice and say how I should be / But they're twisted and they will never be / Any influence on me."

The same goes for "The Last Day of Our Acquaintance," inspired by O'Connor's late 1989 breakup with manager Fachtna O'Ceallaigh, with whom she'd been having an affair even though she married John Reynolds after Jake's birth. For all the sage advice O'Ceallaigh had given her about standing up to the label, she came to see him as a controlling Svengali—their personal and professional relationship summarized by a single devastating line: "I'll talk but you won't listen."

I Do Not Want What I Haven't Got wasn't just an album. It was O'Connor's plea for the freedom and space to grow and become her own person. Yet despite all the courage it took to go after that goal, it was overshadowed, perhaps even eclipsed, by the attention around a single song that had been suggested to her by O'Ceallaigh, who likely saw it as an opportunity for a hit single. He was both right and wrong.

When audiences first heard that "Nothing Compares 2 U" was penned by Prince, many mistakenly thought O'Connor was just another of his many protégés, and many still do. In fact, "Nothing Compares 2 U" wasn't even known as a Prince song when she put it out, and it was never a major song in his repertoire. It was first recorded and released by one of his side projects, The Family, in 1985, and went absolutely nowhere. This was the same year O'Connor signed her recording contract with Ensign, before anyone outside of Ireland knew who she was.

Prince didn't release his own version of "Nothing Compares 2 U" as a single until 1993—as a duet with Rosie Gaines, who actually *was* one of his protégés. This was three years *after* O'Connor put it on the map, it blew up, and it became her signature song. Prince played no part in mentoring her career, her decision to sing the song, its arrangement, its recording, or its release. All he did was cash the check for the songwriting royalties, a business transaction that entailed the personal involvement of neither party.

The album's title, *I Do Not Want What I Haven't Got*, was a reference to a dream in which O'Connor's mother acknowledged that she could not be forgiven for the way she had abused her. Yet O'Connor's take on "Nothing Compares 2 U" sounds as though that's precisely what she's offering. Abandoned and aggrieved, she infuses the song with her own heartbreak and sensibilities, telling her mother, "I'm willing to give it another try."

John Maybury brought that all out in the music video. O'Connor appears in a simple black turtleneck, her face framed in an extreme close-up. As she sings, her eyes appear sad, then angry, then hurt, and searching. When she gets to the line "All the flowers that you planted, Mama, in the backyard, all died when you went away," O'Connor thought of her own mother and began to cry, an expression of sorrow that couldn't be faked, not on any director's cue, not by even the most talented actor.

Thanks to round-the-clock rotation of that video on MTV, O'Connor could no longer simply be dismissed or discounted, distorted as an enigma, or portrayed as a slutty little rap-loving scamp clutching her boombox. As critic Hilton Als pointed out, "Hers [was] a face meant to play on the big screen of our imagination, the only contemporary star we have who could carry a silent film on the strength of her expressive visage and countenance."[2]

That face, cinematic and iconic, propelled O'Connor to global fame. Her follow-up single, "The Emperor's New Clothes," quickly took the top spot on the modern rock chart, followed by a 12-inch remix by Public Enemy producer Hank Shocklee. Another song on the album, "Jump in the River," had already been picked up for the 1988 *Married to the Mob* soundtrack, and a 12-inch remix followed featuring a cameo from the performance artist Karen Finley. O'Connor was tapped for an all-star performance of Pink Floyd's *The Wall*, an Elton John tribute album, and a compilation to benefit AIDS charities. She made her acting debut in the Irish film *Hush-a-Bye Baby*. And so on . . .

But as she ascended as a superstar, it also became clearer that she was stubbornly unwilling to say and do the things that being a superstar required. In fact, she did the opposite, often saying and doing things that were forbidden. O'Connor was a nonconformist, a contrarian even, yet as Als points out, we still demanded "that she remain silent so that we can continue to feed our imagination, not have to deal with her as fully realized person with wants, needs, desires, and viewpoints, least of all those which challenge the status quo or call out our complicity."[3]

Foreshadowing what was soon to come, O'Connor started wearing a green T-shirt at her concerts that read P.W.A.—which stood for "Paddies with attitude." Her first overt breach of pop protocol came in May 1990, only two months after the release of *I Do Not Want What I Haven't Got*. After learning that Andrew Dice Clay, who was known for misogynistic and homophobic humor, was lined up to host *SNL*, O'Connor pulled out of her highly publicized appearance as a musical guest on the same episode. Rather than being respected for her taking a stand against misogyny and homophobia, she was widely criticized for "censoring" the comedian.[4]

Two months later, the accusation was leveled again. There are two versions of this story that have floated around for years. In the first, which has been told by O'Connor's guitarist Marco Pirroni, O'Connor learned that the Garden State Arts Center customarily played the national anthem before shows and protested because she didn't feel the song had anything to do with her music, and she didn't like other people telling her what to do.

In the other version, which she has told several times, O'Connor was approached backstage right before a show at New Jersey's Garden State Arts Center by two people posing as news reporters. Believing that she was being interviewed about her preferences, she told them she'd rather not have the national anthem played before she took the stage. The fake reporters thanked her, wished her well, then called a local TV news show claiming that O'Connor had threatened to cancel the concert if the song was played.

In either case, the song was played *and* the show went off without a hitch. Still, O'Connor was criticized for "censoring" the national anthem, banned from future shows at the Garden State Arts Center, and blacklisted by several local radio stations. When Frank Sinatra performed at the Garden State Arts Center the following night, he told the audience he wished he could meet O'Connor so he could "kick her ass."

Unsure of how to manage the situation, O'Connor attempted to defuse it, telling *Esquire* that she wouldn't be able to hit Sinatra back because she would probably kill the septuagenarian. Her father made similar jokes, bragging to reporters about how she could kick Sinatra's ass.[5] The strategy backfired royally and was used as ammunition against O'Connor by Republican New York state senator Nicholas Spano, who urged a boycott of O'Connor's upcoming show at the Saratoga Arts Center.[6]

DJ Scott Lonsberry of WQBK-AM in Albany piled on, calling O'Connor a fascist and Nazi.[7] Shortly after that, she was approached in a Beverly Hills grocery store by the clerk, who started shouting the national anthem in her face. When he was fired for harassing her, O'Connor's detractors falsely claimed that she had incited him to do it.[8]

O'Connor was no longer simply written off as a troubled child. She was recast as an angry woman, an outsider who was anti-American and ungrateful for her success. Fueling this revision was the growing realization that she posed a much greater threat than merely being a dick tease to guys like Legs McNeil. She was a kick in the crotch.

Even more threatening, her music was dark, personal, and deeply understood by those who had been showing up to her arena concerts, including throngs of young women with their heads shaved, tapping into the powerful energy she was emitting.

In that resistance O'Connor found a *raison d'être*. She was finally being recognized as the protest singer she had always wanted to be. She knew that her willingness to express herself authentically, and without the slightest concern for professional self-preservation, made her dangerous, but also powerful. All Andrew Dice Clay could do in the face of it was to call her "the bald chick." All Frank Sinatra could do was to call her "a stupid broad." Those were just names. She'd experienced and survived far worse than that.

THE TAKEDOWN

Whenever O'Connor was attacked in or by the press, she responded by doubling, or sometimes even tripling, down. She saw others' attempts to silence her not merely as gate-keeping, but as suppression. She likened her experience to the censorship faced by rap artists, whose music and videos the industry power brokers would not play, whose award ceremonies they would not televise, whose music represented an unacceptable threat to the power they held, often without question.

It wasn't long before she had an opportunity to make that connection explicit. Shortly before the Garden State Arts Center incident, a Florida federal district court judge had ruled that 2 Live Crew's album *As Nasty as They Wanna Be* was "obscene" and banned the band from performing live. When they were arrested for defying the order, O'Connor came out publicly in strong support of the rap group, calling out the judge's ban as racially motivated.[1]

In stark contrast to her early interviews just a few years before, by 1990 O'Connor had grown her audience and had become far more outspoken. When MTV's Kurt Loder mansplained to her that sexism was prevalent in a lot of rap music, O'Connor called out the double standard that gave sexist white artists such as Billy Idol, Warrant, and Aerosmith a pass while refusing airplay to Black artists.[2]

As a double slap, she added that rap music was better and often more intelligent.

When she told Loder that she thought rap and hip-hop were regarded as threats because they were so popular, Loder became visibly tense and tried to argue back that some people find rap lyrics offensive. O'Connor shut him down by pointing out that those people don't have to listen to it.

Without other bullets to fire, Loder then turned to the question of motherhood, asking whether it might prevent O'Connor from achieving her full potential. She countered that it grounded her in something real, pointing out that the world of rock stardom is not real. When he asked about the Garden State Arts Center controversy, and suggested that she had offended Sinatra, O'Connor restated her position, biting back at Loder that Sinatra may have needed some publicity.

All of this was building up to the 1990 MTV Video Music Awards, which were hosted by Arsenio Hall at the peak of his fame.[3] In his opening monologue, Hall wound his way through the aisles of the auditorium, bragging that the broadcast was being beamed to more than a hundred countries around the world. Pointing out various celebrities to the camera, he upped the energy, pumped up the crowd.

O'Connor could have easily used the show to promote her own celebrity. In addition to beating Madonna by winning for "Best Female Music Video" and "Best Postmodern Music Video," O'Connor also swept "Video of the Year" for "Nothing Compares 2 U."

O'Connor seemed genuinely stunned. Aside from thanks, she said almost nothing when she was presented with the first two trophies. But when she was presented with the third, she used her speech to connect her experience with the censorship of Black artists.[4]

Explaining her reasons for not wanting the national anthem played before her shows, O'Connor told the live global audience, "It's the [American] system I have disrespect for, which imposes censorship on people, which as far as I'm concerned is racism. I didn't want to go onstage after the national anthem of a country that's harassing people when they perform at gigs." O'Connor then dug in even deeper, calling attention to how MTV used "obscenity" as an excuse not to play rap videos, stating that "censorship in any form is bad, but when it's racism disguised as censorship, it's even worse."

Shortly after the MTV Awards, O'Connor was honored again, this time by *Billboard* as 1990 Artist of the Year in a televised ceremony, where the award was presented by Joni Mitchell.[5] O'Connor appeared grateful, but again refrained from simply offering the typical thank-yous.

Instead, she explained to the crowd that *I Do Not Want What I Haven't Got* exposed her to more happiness and pain than she imagined existed in the world. She expressed gratitude for being able to communicate with people on an emotional level, but she also spoke of the pain that came from not being accepted on a human level by those in the industry and the media.

Even though this was probably not what the audience expected, they cheered as she thanked her friends, her son, and God. Then, rather than plugging the record that made her "artist of the year," she held up a CD: a compilation of Cole Porter covers released as a benefit for AIDS charities. She used the rest of her speech to raise AIDS awareness, then walked across the stage and started singing "You Do

Something to Me," ending by telling the audience, "Thank you very much, wear a condom!"

In 1990, this was a very big deal. Pop stars were expected to get up and sing and, if they were women, to look sexy while doing it. They were not supposed to use their platform to point out societal problems or to advocate for change. O'Connor's actions were seen by industry power players as not only an expression of her ingratitude for her stardom but tantamount to biting the hand that had fed her. Soon afterward, her personal life became tabloid fodder.

As her marriage to John Reynolds was coming to an end, stories started circulating that she had become involved with Hugh Harris, a Black singer who opened for her on tour. The rumored source was Jake's nanny, who is said to have been paid to dish the dirt. O'Connor responded by telling *Rolling Stone* that her personal life was no one's business, but when speculation followed that she was pregnant with Harris's baby, Harris left the tour.[6]

At the same time reports started surfacing about a bizarre run-in with Prince. After "Nothing Compares 2 U" became a huge 1990 hit, he invited O'Connor to his Hollywood megamansion. In her memoir, O'Connor relays that she thought perhaps he wanted to celebrate with her. Her friends speculated that it might be a date, which she would have been open to. It turned out to be neither.[7]

In O'Connor's account, Prince told her that he didn't approve of her cursing in her interviews, and when she told him to fuck off, he lost his composure. He appeared to get over it, but then strangely started a pillow fight. When he whacked her in the head, she could tell something hard was stuffed inside. She fled from his house in the middle of the night, out to the unlit grounds and into the street, where she was finally able to phone a friend for help.

In 1990, it was no secret within the industry that Prince was a control freak, but he was also widely regarded as a musical genius and an ally to women. Plus, he had raked in about $70 million in gross revenues from his 1984 film *Purple Rain*, and six of his albums cracked the *Billboard* Top 10. Despite the significant commercial success of *I Do Not Want What I Haven't Got*, O'Connor was not nearly as powerful as Prince. Plus, she was widely regarded as that uptight bitch who hated men and America.

Anticipating the backlash that always seemed to follow her whenever she told people things they didn't want to hear, O'Connor kept the story under wraps, telling only a few people, including her new manager, Steve Fargnoli, who had previously managed Prince from 1979 until Prince abruptly fired him a decade later without explanation.

Fargnoli believed O'Connor, even speculating that the attack might have been motivated by the bad blood between the two men. O'Connor didn't want to be involved. She wanted to pretend the assault had never happened, that most of what happened that year had never happened. She couldn't seem to get a break.[8]

By December 1990, O'Connor found herself trying to explain many of her previous missteps with the press, telling a reporter from the *Los Angeles Times* that "we all learn as we go along. I've done all my growing up in public." She went on to discuss at length having been abused as a child and how it informed the way she felt helpless and alone when no one intervened or asked why she was acting out. As she explained, "The result was I was made to feel I was a terrible person. The real problem was brushed under the carpet."[9]

This insight is so honest, and feels so tragic, because that pattern would continue no matter how many times or how hard she tried to stop it. O'Connor always seemed to be looking for a sympathetic ear, someone to help her reframe so that her ideas were the focus — not her haircut or who she was sleeping with.

O'Connor had seen Madonna on Arsenio Hall's talk show, which was at that time the hottest TV show on late night. Hall seemed to treat Madonna with respect, even when she teased him about his old flame, Paula Abdul. In general, Hall's banter with guests seemed easygoing — maybe he was just the ticket she was looking for.

Hall began his interview with O'Connor by joking about how they had both been criticized for their haircuts. That didn't land particularly well, but he smoothly segued into asking O'Connor about her work on the AIDS charity compilation.[10]

It should have been a softball since ostensibly that's what O'Connor was there to promote, but she appeared nervous, and awkwardly asked Hall what he wanted to know. Anything she thought the audience should know about the album, he replied, but O'Connor struggled for an answer. Hall seemed sensitive, gently suggesting that there was probably something relevant to the cause that she wanted to talk about.

"Well, what it is," O'Connor began to mumble, and then, without taking a breath, she started an extended monologue, "is a collection of Cole Porter songs, uh, and it's done by a whole collection of artists."

She went on to name-check a few, then rambled on in a hushed monotone about the necessity of AIDS education and the idea that people are more likely to listen to musicians than politicians. Hall frowned, looking for a chance to break in. Then she finally landed on an applause line:

"They don't want to hear what Margaret Thatcher has to say about it. They don't want to know about what she has to say about anything. . . ."

O'Connor smiled, and Hall said he was glad because he wasn't sure the audience could hear what she was saying. O'Connor played with her hands and apologized for speaking quietly, taking in the criticism. Hall took the opening to steer the interview in a different direction, to familiar ground that would play well with his audience.

He brought up Andrew Dice Clay and the Garden State Arts Center controversies, asking O'Connor what she would like people to know and understand about her. She responded in a subdued tone, "That I'm a human being. That I'm not a rock star and that I don't want to be treated like one and I don't want to be looked up to as being one. It's an accident that I'm famous. I didn't set out to be. It just so happens that 'Nothing Compares 2 U' did really well."

She went on to echo what she told the reporter from the *Los Angeles Times*. "So, what I would say is I'm a human being, and as such I'm very young, and as a result of being famous I've had to do all of my growing up in public, you know what I mean? So, there will be bound to be things that I'll do, and I'm not referring to the national anthem thing, that I will later regret. There are bound to be things that I would do in a different way now than I did six months ago, do you know what I mean? That's life. But I'm a human being, that's all."

Hall pressed her on what specifically she would do differently. O'Connor sighed, then reiterated her position on the national anthem while expressing regret that people saw her decision to pull out of *SNL* as censoring Andrew Dice Clay. Hall then moved to rap, pointing out that songs by artists such as 2 Live Crew and N.W.A. have sexist lyrics. O'Connor smiled a little, explaining that "as a girl" she liked those songs but also saw how others might find them offensive.

Hall pushed back on O'Connor's claim that she never sought fame, and she tried to explain that wanting to sing and be heard isn't the same as desiring stardom. The audience's applause suggested that they understood the distinction, but not Hall himself. He dismissively said, "Yeah, yeah," before returning to the backlash, asking O'Connor how she managed it.

It's frustrating to watch this exchange, to see O'Connor walk right back into the same old trap. She tried to counter the misperception that she courts negativity, pointing out that anyone who knows her or sees her trying to explain herself in interviews understands that she isn't angry or aggressive. She added that she was flattered that Frank Sinatra even knew who she was. Hall cut to commercial, and when they returned something very strange happened.

Hall asked O'Connor about "Black Boys on Mopeds." Rather than talking about Bramble or Roach, or the broader issue of police violence against young Black men, O'Connor replied with an awkward joke about wanting to release the song as a single with a photo of her half-naked on the cover, and a question mark over the image, which she then described as an invitation for Black boys to come over on mopeds . . .

What was happening here? Why was she suddenly sexualizing the interview? Was this a response to counter the public's misperceptions about her anger and negativity? Was she trying to disarm Hall by making herself appear sexually available?

Hall seemed shocked, then asked whether the song

wasn't about combating racism. She described it as wanting to address the problem of racism from the maternal point of view, explaining that she'd heard that a sixteen-year-old boy was killed in a police chase, and his mother was abused when she attended a protest. But just as she began to make this serious point, O'Connor defused it, shifting back to sexualizing the exchange: "But I also wanted to see if there were any good-looking men out there who wanted to . . ."

Hall was perplexed and visibly embarrassed. He abruptly changed the topic, asking O'Connor about her son Jake and the pressure she says the label placed on her to end her pregnancy. She confirmed the story, reiterating that she had the right to make choices about her own body. He asked about a rumor that she once wanted to be a nun; she confirmed that she did until she learned that she couldn't have sex. They ended the segment with a light discussion about her stint as a kiss-o-gram girl, where she cracked the old jokes from her earliest American interviews.

Things went even worse in her next exchange with *SPIN*'s Legs McNeil. This time, McNeil's profile acknowledged that 1990 had been the "Year of O'Connor," but after mentioning her string of accomplishments, he went right on to talk about himself.[11]

Without explaining how he came to have an inside scoop, McNeil bragged about how other reporters offered him money in exchange for intel on which guys O'Connor was sleeping with, how he'd even discussed the matter with his mother. Their discussion was openly racist, making much of public speculation that O'Connor was into Black men at a time when the Gallup poll reported that less than 50 percent of the American public approved of interracial marriage.[12]

From there, McNeil went on to recap every controversy

that O'Connor had been embroiled in that year, then pivoted to his appearance as a guest on a radio show where he was asked to respond to listeners who called in to complain about her. Here are some of the statements McNeil says he made in O'Connor's defense:

> Sinéad's 23 years old and from Dublin; she doesn't look for headlines. It's almost an accident that she's as big as she is.
>
> Sinéad's a delightful person, she's really a sweetheart, and I think she's a little overwhelmed at what has happened to her, and I think she's trying to maintain who she is, and I think it comes off. . . .

We don't hear a single word from O'Connor herself until the very end, where they're inexplicably together in a hotel room. McNeil says she's looking "as dreamy as ever." They proceed to flirt, and McNeil asks her if she is ready to accept being a rock star. Preempting her response, McNeil recounts how he recently defended O'Connor on the radio show, and presents her with transcripts to prove it, telling O'Connor that "chivalry is not dead." She thanks him.

Then McNeil asks her how she felt about the Garden State Arts Center. She stands her ground, remarking that she has nothing to apologize for. Ditto for her decision to boycott *SNL*. When McNeil tries to call her out for censorship, she deftly articulates the difference between deciding not to appear on the same stage with the comedian and the way that MTV censors Black artists while holding white artists to a different standard.

For a brief moment, they appeared to be heading into an actual conversation, but McNeil wouldn't let it go there. "New subject," he said. "It's been a hell of a year for you.

And you've missed me terribly." O'Connor replied, "Oh, I've been aching for you, Legs, of course."

Did this really happen? If so, was McNeil's self-flattering joke about how much she missed him the moment where O'Connor finally realized that her interviews were a sucker's game? She wanted to talk about misogyny and racism and the AIDS crisis, even though the message didn't always get through. They wanted her to shut the hell up unless she was singing, or in McNeil's case, coming on to them, or at least that they could say that she did.

Whatever tactics she used to navigate that minefield, what remained was the rage. When the Grammy nominations were announced in January 1991, *I Do Not Want What I Haven't Got* was up for four categories, including Record of the Year, Best Female Pop Vocal Performance, Best Music Video, Short Form, and Best Alternative Music Performance.

Other artists might have seen these nominations as validation, but after the past year, O'Connor just didn't care anymore. She wrote a letter to the Recording Academy explaining that she would not accept an award if she were given one and criticizing the industry for promoting false and materialistic values rather than rewarding artistic merit.

"They respect mostly material gain, since that is the main reason for their existence," part of her letter read, "and they have created a great respect among artists for material gain—by honoring us and exalting us when we achieve it, ignoring for the most part those of us who have not."

Again, O'Connor came out and said the true thing no one wanted to hear. Well, almost no one. When the nominee for "Best Rap Performance by a Duo or Group," Public Enemy, learned about O'Connor's letter, the band decided to boycott the Grammy Awards ceremony, too, making a statement about the Recording Academy's ongoing refusal to broadcast the presentation of the award, and returning the solidarity she had offered them in 1989. When Living Colour guitarist Vernon Reid accepted his Grammy for "Best Hard Rock Performance," he appeared on stage with a giant photo of O'Connor on his shirt.

As for O'Connor herself, as she promised, she did not come to the ceremony to collect the award for "Best Alternative Music Performance." Instead, she spent the evening watching the show on TV at Eddie Murphy's house, as a guest of Arsenio Hall.

She had appeared on Hall's show again the previous night, where she explained her decision to forgo music awards altogether.[13] Hall expressed respect for her position, even fawning admiration. They flirted a bit. Overall, the mood was much more relaxed than it had been during her first appearance, at least until Hall asked her about Prince, referencing the assault without disclosing the details.

O'Connor seemed surprised and clearly didn't want to talk about it. Hall cut away to a commercial, and when they returned, he reintroduced O'Connor, who began to perform an a capella version of a song written by John Gibbs and originally recorded by the Irish Celtic rock band Moving Hearts.

Called "Irish Ways and Irish Laws," it's a sad but beautiful tale of oppression, awakening, and resilience. O'Connor's singing gave it a different kind of energy. Startlingly sparse and intense, it sent chills up your spine and landed like a shudder.

Whatever was said that year about O'Connor as a person — that she was a troubled child, that she was anti-American, that she was angry and ungrateful, that she was bald, and freaky, and profane — in that moment no one could deny the grace and beauty and sheer force of her voice.

When she finished, the crowd went wild with applause and O'Connor broke into a smile, knowing that, at least for the moment, she had overcome all the bullshit. Arsenio Hall's invitation to Eddie Murphy's party probably felt like an olive branch, a way of saying he understood that she was an artist. But years later O'Connor would claim that Hall had spiked her drink.[14]

IS SHE NOT YOUR GIRL?

Most pop stars would have reset from a terrible year of highs and lows by staying out of sight for a while or rushing out an album of crowd-pleasing hits. But O'Connor's next effort was the 1991 offering *My Special Child*, a four-song EP intended to raise awareness about child abuse. In her press interviews, she was vocal about her own experiences as an abuse survivor, telling *SPIN*'s Bob Guccione Jr. that she considered child abuse to be the cause of all the world's problems.[1]

O'Connor went on to identify the role of education and other forms of social conditioning in discouraging children from formulating their own viewpoints, from becoming their own people, and from learning how to advocate for themselves. She implicated television, telling Guccione Jr. that she specifically believed MTV should be abolished for promoting the wrong values. When he pointed out that MTV had played a significant role in exposing her as an artist, she didn't waver from her position.

When you look back at this interview, the clash of interests is glaring. She wants to use her fame to help abused children. He wants to use her fame to sell magazines. Talking about child abuse does not sell magazines, so although Guccione Jr. gave O'Connor a platform to express her views, he also editorialized them.

Calling the profile "Special Child," he blurred the title of her EP with a reference to O'Connor herself, part of a burgeoning "Sinéad is crazy" narrative that was starting to appear everywhere, perpetuated even by those who had previously appeared to support her—including Arsenio Hall.

The culture condoned it, and even demanded it. Women were often on board with the takedown, even "edgy" self-declared feminists, such as the multi-hyphenate comedian-actress-singer Sandra Bernhard. Ever since Bernhard started appearing as a regular on David Letterman's show in the late 1980s, she had been sharpening her mean-girl shtick, which was centered on expressing her "uncensored" opinions about headlining celebrities. But when she appeared as a guest on Arsenio Hall's show in November 1991, their routine was particularly cruel:[2]

AH: I know you wrote to Frank and Sinéad when they had problems.

SB: Right, well I was concerned about both of them.

AH: (Laughs along with the audience.)

SB, tapping AH: I heard Prince beat up Sinéad or something? (She makes a "sheesh" face.)

AH: That's what she said. I haven't talked to Prince yet.

SB: I couldn't be happier.

(Laughter from Hall and the audience.)

SB: Prince is back and better than ever and kicking Sinéad's butt.

(She raises her hand and swings it back and forth in a smacking motion.)

SB: Why, you little bald-headed . . .

AH: Well, what do you think of her stance . . .

SB: Freaky cue-balled freak!

(Audience laughter and cheers.)

SB: What do I think of her stance?

AH: Yeah.

SB: Which one?

(She makes a purse-lipped, angry face.)

SB: The Lions will lay down with the lambs.

AH: The latest one, with the Grammys.

SB: What did she do with the Grammys?

AH: Ah, well she's not going to accept one and she's not going to go.

SB: Okay, well, then, she won't get one.

AH: (Laughs.) Simple as that!

SB: I don't get it with Sinéad-y.

(Laughter.)

SB: She's so pretty with some hair, I mean with a wig, just throw a wig on her.

AH: Well, she did put on a blond wig . . .

SB: Send her home. She's so miserable here I don't know why she wants to stay.

(Laughter and hoots.)

SB: I'll tell you what, Sinéad, I'll go to Ireland and make as much money as you're making here and I'll be happy.

(Cheers.)

AH: That's a good point.

O'Connor also made fashion czar Mr. Blackwell's list of worst dressed women, where he referred to her as "the bald-headed banshee of MTV" and "a new age nightmare." MC Hammer jumped on the bandwagon, telling the *Los Angeles Times* that he'd pay for O'Connor to "go home." After six months in Los Angeles, she had already planned to go to England to be closer to Jake and his father, so O'Connor publicly sent Hammer the $2,600 bill for the plane ticket.

Making a practice of showing that she would not be intimidated or shamed, O'Connor went to a bookstore with *Rolling Stone* reporter David Wild in tow, purchasing a copy of her unauthorized biography while explaining, "I don't do anything in order to cause trouble. It just so happens that what I do causes trouble. And that's fine with me. I'm *proud* to be a troublemaker."[3]

In his interview, Wild referenced O'Connor's accusations against Prince, which he described as "unpleasant experiences." Aside from saying that "the experiences" made her no longer want to perform "Nothing Compares 2 U," O'Connor didn't take the bait from him. She also never hit back directly at those who mocked her, instead focusing on what she thought mattered most: drawing attention to her music.

For her next album, O'Connor chose to record a collection of show tunes and standards that were tied to childhood memories. Her mother's record collection was vast, and O'Connor would often sing to calm her nerves. "Don't Cry for Me Argentina" was one of her mother's favorites. Her father used to serenade young O'Connor with "Scarlet Ribbons." As with "Nothing Compares 2 U," O'Connor brought her own sensibilities to the repertoire, recentering the meanings of these songs in the context of her personal and family history.

In place of Loretta Lynn's country spin, O'Connor arranged the album's lead single, "Success Has Made a Failure of Our Home," with strings and brass. At times it sounds as if the instruments will overwhelm her voice, but it grows stronger with every verse, quaking until it begins to soar. Toward the end of the song, O'Connor pleads "Stop what you're saying, you're killing me." Repeatedly she asks the addressee "Am I Not Your Girl?" until the whole song collapses, seemingly in exhaustion.

The closing track offered listeners something even darker: a hidden spoken-word track entitled "Personal Message about Pain (Jesus and the Money Changers)." O'Connor begins with the statement: "I am not a liar and I'm not full of hatred, but I hate liars and so the liars hate me." She follows with a hushed question: "Can you really say you're not in pain like me?" She then warns the listener of an impending holy war that will necessitate great sacrifice and death. She leaves no question as to the identity of the enemy, whom she describes as "the one wearing the collar."

This was very intense stuff, and for the most part it was too much for the critics. *Rolling Stone*'s Elyse Gardner gave *Am I Not Your Girl?* a devastating two-star review, charging that O'Connor tried too hard for "demure understatement" and "has yet to display the emotional authority required of a great chanteuse."[4] Robert Christgau was even harsher in his assessment, explaining that the album "stiffed because no one understood it, possibly including O'Connor."[5]

On the contrary, I'd say O'Connor understood it quite well and didn't care if it stiffed. Her commitments were apparent in the music video for "Success Has Made a Failure of Our Home," where she stands at a dais testifying about child abuse (via sign language).[6] On the wall behind O'Connor appear the faces of children on slides from Amnesty International—the young victims of war atrocities. As a personal lament becomes a battle cry against an unforgivable crime against humanity, photographers flash photographs of the event, confusing her statement with entertainment.

Her point was that this was not entertainment, and she had no interest in being an entertainer or pushing units. As far as O'Connor was concerned, the world was suffering from spiritual deprivation, and the only antidote was truth-telling, no matter the cost to her or her career.

She made that clear to Guccione Jr. when she said of her critics and detractors, "They know that I'm not one in a million. I'm merely expressing the feelings of millions of people. I just have a platform to air those views, and I'm operating for loads of people. I'm operating for all the abused children and all the women and all of the people who have been completely and utterly oppressed."

God had saved her so she could save them, or so it might have seemed. And so it was that on October 3, 1992, O'Connor took a significant step toward an outcome that she understood as a *fait accompli*.

THIS MEANS WAR

It's important to note that all of this played out in the context of monoculture, when the eyes of the world could be simultaneously focused on a single event. For *SNL*'s 1992–1993 season, that meant 12.7 million viewers tuned in to each episode — take a moment to assess that breathtaking number.[1]

When O'Connor appeared as the musical guest on October 3, 1992, she performed "Success Has Made a Failure of Our Home" for her first set. For her second, she chose something that was not on her new album: Bob Marley's 1976 song "War."

This was not a random selection, or a particularly well-known song, so let's break it down. First, the lyrics to "War" are a nearly verbatim recital of a speech made by the Ethiopian emperor Haile Selassie before the General Assembly of the United Nations in 1963. A cry for peace and demand for the recognition of equality among all races, classes, and nations, it states that until the day that equality is reached there will be war. Selassie closes expressing confidence in the victory of good over evil.

When O'Connor took to the stage to perform "War," she intended to stand in solidarity with that view. Her microphone stand was draped with a scarf in the Rastafari colors of green, gold, and red. She wore a white beaded dress with a Rasta Star of David pendant around her neck.

The Star of David was a reference to the Rastafari belief that there is a direct genetic line from Kings David and Solomon to Selassie. Therefore, Rastas saw him not only as a head of state but also as the incarnation of God.

Rastas also held that the Catholic Church condoned slavery and promoted the colonization of Africa. O'Connor believed that, too, and further came to believe that the Catholic Church was complicit in the perpetuation of child abuse. Right before the show, O'Connor went so far as to tell a reporter from the British magazine *Vox* that she believed the Church *wanted* children to be abused. "That's why they want to ban abortion," O'Connor said. "Because unless we're being abused, they don't have any power — we don't reach out to them."[2]

During the dress rehearsal O'Connor disclosed to *SNL* producers that she intended to perform "War" and that at the end she would hold up a picture of a street kid who'd been killed by the cops. But when it was showtime, and she came out to sing a breathtaking a capella version of Marley's "War," she went further in establishing the links she saw by altering some of the lyrics to directly address the evils of child abuse.

O'Connor paused briefly at the end and reached for a large photograph of Pope John Paul II. She held it up to the camera, staring intensely at the lens, then sustained the word "evil" before ripping the photograph to shreds, and proclaiming "Fight the real enemy!"

O'Connor then blew out some nearby candles and left the stage, leaving the audience in stunned silence. She hastily made her way back to her dressing room, then left the building with her personal assistant. Two people egged them on the street. The next day NBC received more than five hundred complaints from viewers, then four hundred more on Monday. Only seven people called to defend O'Connor.

Some viewers misrecognized her Rasta Star of David as a Jewish star.[3] The Anti-Defamation League immediately distanced itself from O'Connor, putting out a statement that her disrespect of the pope was deplorable. A spokesperson for Marley's family and foundation did not defend her directly, stating only that in a democracy she had the right to her own interpretation of the speech and the song.

Most people watching at home that night missed that O'Connor was taking a bold stand against racism, colonialism, and child abuse; everyone was laser-focused on those last few seconds of the performance. That was enough to draw their fury.

O'Connor was not the first person to call out the Catholic Church on the brewing child abuse crisis. As early as September 1983, the progressive newspaper *National Catholic Reporter* reported on abuse cases in Portland, Oregon, though they appeared to involve a single priest.[4] Two years later, a news report involving a Louisiana priest was picked up by the national press, but again, it appeared to be isolated. No one had gone before millions of TV viewers to suggest that the problem was widespread or systemic, or that the Church had not only condoned it but also covered it up. Certainly, no one destroyed a photo of the pope to make those points.

A conservative group that called itself the National Ethnic Coalition of Organizations organized a widely publicized event where O'Connor's albums were steamrollered outside of Chrysalis's offices in Rockefeller Center.⁵ They also promised to donate $10 to charity for every tape or CD that was destroyed by others, and to send the remains to O'Connor.

Although that turned out to be an empty threat, the *New York Post* declared O'Connor "A HOLY TERROR." *Newsday*'s headline read, "No hair, no taste." She faced overwhelming condemnation from a host of celebrities, including Arsenio Hall, who invited a fake pope on his show to tear up a photo of O'Connor, and Phil Hartman, who joked on *David Letterman* about tearing up a photo of her supposed lookalike, Uncle Fester, the hairless hunched character from the *Addams Family*. Camille Paglia was perhaps the harshest of all, proclaiming that "in her case child abuse was justified."⁶

Everyone expected to hear from Madonna. Although her rivalry with O'Connor was largely cooked up by the press, dubbed Blond Ambition versus Bald Ambition, there was some truth to it. Or at least Madonna played along with it, mocking O'Connor's appearance by telling reporters that she looked like she'd had a run-in with a lawnmower, and was as sexy as a Venetian blind.

But this time she needed a different approach. Like O'Connor, Madonna had rejected the marketing dictates of her record label, but unlike O'Connor, Madonna had used her sexuality and religious roots to sell herself.⁷

From the outset, Madonna's promotional strategy was to subvert her Catholic upbringing, starting with her single-word name, given to her by her devout mother, who died when she was seven. First, Madonna paired crucifixes with lingerie. Then she made "Papa Don't Preach," about a teen girl who discloses an unplanned pregnancy to her father.

When the Catholic Church fervently objected to that, she stepped it up even more, baiting and outraging cultural conservatives.

When her four-year marriage to actor Sean Penn was ending in 1989, Madonna publicly hinted at a lesbian relationship with Sandra Bernhard, which they played up during a joint appearance on *David Letterman*. In her video for "Like a Prayer," Madonna featured burning crosses, interracial sexualized scenes with a Black Jesus-like saint, dancing inside of a church, and even stigmata.

The conservative American Family Association condemned her, as did Pepsi, which pulled out of a lucrative commercial deal. But Madonna's bold gambles paid off, the attention generating free publicity for her carefully staged pseudoscandals. They worked because, unlike O'Connor's, Madonna's blasphemy was playful, a wink that bordered on camp.

Madonna's 1990 "Blond Ambition" tour took her to fifty-seven cities around the world, where she sang and danced for an audience of about 800,000 people. When she performed "Like a Prayer," she threw simulated masturbation into the mix, along with a faux Mass on a stage that was adorned with stained-glass windows and religious symbolism. She and her dancers wore liturgical costumes designed by Jean Paul Gaultier. Instead of having her records steamrollered by religious conservatives, she raked in just shy of $63 million (roughly $124 million in today's dollars).

All of this is to say that for the first decade of her career, Madonna not only anticipated but courted controversy, prevailing by always knowing where the line was and managing to stay one step ahead. What Madonna probably did not anticipate, however, was the arrival of Sinéad O'Connor, whose authenticity was more subversive than any spectacle.[8]

To pretend that she was outraged by O'Connor's *SNL* appearance, or to dismiss it as a publicity stunt, would have been not only hypocritical but also untruthful. Worse, the public would have seen right through it. So, when the Irish public radio network RTÉ approached Madonna, the best she could come up with was: "I think there is a better way to present her ideas rather than ripping up an image that means a lot to other people," adding, "If she is against the Roman Catholic Church and she has a problem with them, I think she should talk about it."[9]

O'Connor did talk about it. Within days, she released an open letter that connected her history of abuse to the history of the Irish people, lobbing a direct attack on the Catholic Church, "[which] has controlled us by controlling education, through their teachings on sexuality, marriage, birth control and abortion, and most spectacularly through the lies they taught us with their history books." O'Connor concluded by reiterating the ideas expressed on the hidden track on *Am I Not Your Girl?*: "My story is the story of countless millions of children whose families and nations were torn apart for money in the name of Jesus Christ."

Robert Christgau had grossly underestimated O'Connor when, in 1990, he dismissed her as a "folkie Madonna."[10] Jon Pareles was the one who had it right when he noted that for all of Madonna's attempts to shock with sex, "O'Connor [had] stole[n] the spotlight with one photograph of a fully-clothed man."[11]

Pareles pointed out that if a male artist or band had torn up a picture of the pope, it would have scarcely made a ripple. Male rebels were lionized, while women were crucified. But more than simply seeing herself as a rebel, O'Connor saw herself as a specific kind of antihero who believed herself to be the "property of Jesus," in the mold of the Christian-era Bob Dylan.

It was Dylan whom O'Connor most emulated, whose music had sustained her through the difficult years of her childhood and adolescence. Dylan knew what it was like to really be misunderstood, rejected, and criticized for who he was—for everything from his appearance to the sound of his voice to his right to make the kind of music he wanted to.

Two weeks after her appearance on *SNL*, O'Connor was thrilled for the opportunity to perform for the man himself, at a four-hour all-star tribute show to be held at Madison Square Garden. The song she chose was "I Believe in You," a deep cut from Dylan's 1979 album *Slow Train Coming*, which her older brother Joseph brought home when she was eleven.

For O'Connor this wasn't just a song about Dylan's belief in God, but a song about her belief in Dylan. After her parents split up and O'Connor's mother forbade her from seeing her father, she played that song over and over. After *SNL*, she didn't care what the haters thought of her as long as Dylan understood:

> They ask me how I feel
> And if my love is real
> And how I know I'll make it through
> And they, they look at me and frown
> They'd like to drive me from this town
> They don't want me around
> 'Cause I believe in you.

As O'Connor was about to take the stage, Kris Kristofferson introduced her as "an artist whose name is synonymous with courage and integrity." But when she came out, some members of the audience booed loudly. Then she was cheered by others who were trying to drown them out. Kristofferson leaned into the mic and said, "Don't let the bastards get you down."

O'Connor intended to perform the song as a whisper, as she thought it was meant to be heard, but she realized she couldn't be heard over the crowd. She paced around the stage for a few minutes, trying to figure out what to do. Then she overheard someone calling for Kristofferson.

At that moment she decided to do what she thought Jesus would have done, perhaps Dylan too. Rather than singing "I Believe in You" she defiantly began shouting the lyrics to Bob Marley's "War," the same song she had performed on *SNL*.

It's so hard for me to watch the SNL episode now. I was at Hampshire College when this all took place. Hardly anyone I knew had a TV, so I only heard about what happened on *SNL* days later. In our classroom, and as young activists, we were no fans of the Church, which we saw as anti-woman, antichoice, and antigay.[12]

So of course our reactions to O'Connor destroying the pope's photo ranged from "So?" or "Good for her." But we were also experiencing these reactions in a bubble, at a tiny liberal arts college in an apple orchard. We didn't have to actually stand up and do it before an audience of millions, nor take the bashing from and in the press, nor appear before 18,000 people at Madison Square Garden, just two weeks later.

If I had been at that Dylan tribute concert fresh off the

bus from Philadelphia, and if I had heard the hecklers boo-ing, I would have seen the faces of my parents. I would have picked a fight with a stranger, fighting back against the pain that was welling inside of me. Isn't that what O'Connor was doing when she started shouting "War"?

When I watch the concert footage now, I see something else. Behind the brave front O'Connor is putting on is the hurt and fear. I can see it in her eyes, the retriggering of the trauma in the audience's boos. When I look at her, I can see myself, my own wounds and scars surfacing. And what I feel now is more sorrow than anger.

Whatever strength she was trying to summon at that moment to hit back, this was not a fair fight. Jesus was not going to appear on a cross on a little stony hill. Dylan was not going to say anything or do anything. My impulse to protect O'Connor is stronger than my desire to destroy them. In that moment, she was on her own.

O'Connor broke down in tears, and Kristofferson escorted her off the stage. Without saying a word about what had just happened, Neil Young swooped in and took her place, jumping into "All Along the Watchtower." I don't know what was going on backstage, but at the end of the show O'Connor reappeared to perform the penulti-mate song along with the other artists. Imagine what cour-age that would have taken, what strength.

After the show Neil Young told the press that he'd been booed before, and it was no big deal—that's why he didn't feel like he needed to defend her. She defended herself in an interview with the *Associated Press*, offering sharp crit-icism of those who booed, pointing out that they failed to get what Dylan was about. However, as a reflection of how deeply it cut, O'Connor also pointed a finger at Dylan himself, suggesting that he was asleep when it happened. She said that after the show Dylan told her to "keep doing what she's doing," but she also expressed disappointment that he didn't take responsibility in that moment and publicly defend her.

In her memoir, she'd reveal that there was a lot more to her reaction than what was reported at the time, more than she was willing to reveal to an unsympathetic public and perhaps even to herself.[13] Directly after the show, O'Connor had also approached Dylan's manager, imploring him to convince Dylan to speak out with her against child abuse. She says it didn't work. He just looked at her as if she were crazy.

And there was her own father, who was in the audience that night, once again witnessing his daughter being attacked and doing nothing. Afterward, he told O'Connor he thought her career had been destroyed and urged her to consider enrolling in college. Was he attempting to shield her from further ridicule, or just throwing up his hands again?

O'Connor wasn't going to give up so fast. Whether or not anyone else saw it, she believed she had a purpose. In 1978, when she was twelve years old and still living with her mother, O'Connor had seen Bob Geldof and the Boomtown Rats on *Top of the Pops*. Reveling in their success at knocking "Summer Nights" off the number-one spot with their song "Rat Trap," Geldof and his bandmates gleefully destroyed photographs of John Travolta before they broke into a performance of their song.[14]

The gesture made a big impression on young O'Connor. Like Dylan, Geldof appeared to be rejecting the notion that pop singers are supposed to shut up and be pretty and sing nice songs. O'Connor felt there had to be a reason that God had spared her life and had given her that voice to sing with. Though she had been treated like a heretic, at least she still had the eyes of the world, and she could still deliver a righteous message.

It's also important to note that the photo of the pope she destroyed on *SNL* was not some random picture of the pontiff. It once hung on the wall in her mother's bedroom, a souvenir of the pope's 1979 visit to Ireland. She always saw it as a symbol of, as she put it, "lies, liars, and abuse." After her mother died, she took the photo and held onto it, intending one day to publicly destroy it, to expose the corruption of the institution.

In the weeks leading up to her appearance on *SNL*, O'Connor had been reading *The Holy Blood and the Holy Grail*, a contrarian history of the early Church, as well as various exposés in Irish newspapers detailing the Church's role in condoning child abuse and discrediting the accounts of survivors.

She knew there would be millions of people watching the show, way more than *Top of the Pops*. She took the photo with her to New York and hid it in her dressing room, thinking of a possible plan. While exploring the city, she overheard a leader of New York's Rasta community remark that "the pope was the devil, and the devil was the real enemy."

Ever since O'Ceallaigh had first introduced her to Rastafarian music and culture in London, O'Connor connected with it profoundly, admiring and emulating its deep spirituality and the way it merged religion and revolutionary politics.[15] When she came to the stage, she was ready to make that statement.

O'Connor chose to sing Bob Marley's "War," hoping to articulate the connection between two kinds of abuse perpetuated by the Catholic Church, a connection largely missed by an audience that was profoundly unaware of the historical, religious, visual, and musical references from which she was drawing. Had they seen that she was also indicting the Church as an enemy of Black liberation, no doubt the vitriol would have been even greater. It would have been seen as tantamount to calling practicing white Catholics racists.

Rather than anticipating the audience's response or being concerned with how it might affect her, O'Connor's only thought was "Nothing can touch me. I reject the world. Nobody can do a thing to me that hasn't been done already."

I believe O'Connor's decision to destroy the photograph was not impulsive or irrational, but instead was triggered by abuse and the need to avenge it. If you read many of the controversial comments she has made, you can see that O'Connor is pushing back against the silence and shame she experienced as a child by telling people things they don't want to hear, even when it opens her up to more shaming and more trauma.

Rather than speculating about whether O'Connor's decision to destroy the photo was self-sabotage, better questions would be: What kinds of sacrifices would she have had to make to sustain her status as a pop star? What price would she have had to pay for obeying the code of silence? Which brings me back to Madonna, with whom I have no personal beef, only disappointment—as much directed toward the culture as the way she negotiated it.

In 1985, when Madonna was among the biggest pop stars in the world, *Playboy* and *Penthouse* published some old nude photos that her ex-boyfriend had taken. Shortly afterward, she came to Philadelphia to perform at Live Aid. When Madonna walked onstage, some people booed and screamed "slut," taunting her to take off her coat. But she defanged them, turning their shaming into a joke, "Nah, I ain't taking shit off today. They might hold it against me ten years from now."

However, 1992 was a different story. Rather than pushing back against the shaming, Madonna chose to shame another woman and turn that silencing to her own advantage. A few months after O'Connor's *SNL* appearance, Madonna appeared on *SNL* to promote her new album, *Erotica*. The song she chose to perform that night was called "Bad Girl." It was an uneventful performance of an unremarkable song, except at the very end. Out of nowhere, Madonna started mimicking O'Connor, proclaiming "Fight the real enemy!" then tearing up a photo of Joey Buttafuoco.

Six months earlier, Buttafuoco's sixteen-year-old lover, Amy Fisher, had shot his wife in the face in a fit of jealousy. Dubbed "the Long Island Lolita" by the tabloids, Fisher was the frequent target of *SNL* parodies, where she was relentlessly trolled as "one messed-up bitch." Meanwhile, the real-life Fisher did seven years in prison for first-degree attempted murder. Buttafuoco denied the affair altogether, then, when he was busted in the lie, he did only a few months for statutory rape.

"Bad Girl" had absolutely nothing to do with advocating on behalf of Fisher, or condemning Buttafuoco's conduct, or making a statement about any of the larger issues. The destruction of the photograph was nothing more than a low blow to O'Connor, a disingenuous grab for attention that was transparent to anyone watching, a rare misstep in an otherwise meticulously orchestrated promotional campaign. I imagine it was something of an embarrassment to Madonna, who never publicly performed the song again. But it did not harm her in any significant way.

While O'Connor was being crucified for being a maverick, Madonna was founding a powerhouse multimedia production company called Maverick. She cut a $60 million deal with Time Warner that gave her unusually tight creative control over a broad range of verticals, including musical recordings, film and television productions, music and book publishing, and insane amounts of merchandising, as well as astronomically high royalty rates.[16]

Erotica was Maverick's first album release. It didn't do as well as Madonna's previous albums, peaking at only number two on the US Billboard 200. But at the same time, Maverick published *Sex*, a glossy coffee-table book featuring explicit images of Madonna engaging in various sexual situations, including taboo practices such as homosexuality, bestiality, and S&M.

The Vatican urged an immediate boycott, calling the content "morally intolerable," which was basically an endorsement as far as Madonna's fanbase was concerned. Even though *Sex* was widely panned by critics and the public, it was nevertheless an instant hit, selling more than 150,000 copies the first day it was available before going on to top 1.5 million copies worldwide.

In 1992, Madonna could have used her voice and power to support O'Connor and Fisher, and all women. Instead, she played into misogyny, aligning herself with it as armor while monetizing her own objectification. That's how Madonna defended her title as the reigning Queen of Pop.

WE DO NOT WANT WHAT SHE HAS GOT

Years later, O'Connor would write in her memoir that *SNL* *rerailed* rather than *derailed* her career, setting it back on the right track, far from the world of pop celebrity.[1] But the reality was a lot more complicated. As O'Connor alternated between retirement and failed comeback attempts, most of her music went unheard, eclipsed by controversial statements, actions, and struggles that often played out in the public eye.

Before *SNL*, O'Connor contributed vocals to Peter Gabriel's 1992 album *Us*. Then in early 1993 she went out on tour with him. They became involved, a relationship that she would describe years later as being used as "weekend pussy."[2] When their affair ended, Gabriel abruptly replaced her on the tour bill with Paula Cole and O'Connor reportedly attempted suicide.

She returned to Ireland, where she fidgeted relentlessly on a TV appearance, telling host Pat Kenny that she had torn up the pope's photo "because she was bored."[3] To some watching, it recalled a radio appearance in the immediate aftermath of *SNL* wherein she had blamed the Catholic Church for Hitler, and described the New Testament as "forgery."[4]

There was also an interview with *Vox* where she went even further, claiming that "the Jews in Germany would not have been exterminated if Hitler had not been abused as a child. Adolf Hitler wasn't a bad person; he was a very [screwed up] person." And in another interview, with *NME*, she said that people were raping their babies, and the only solution to the world's problems was to get rid of money.[5]

More and more people were asking an unavoidable question: Is Sinéad nuts? After Legs McNeil parted ways with *SPIN* in 1993, he launched a tabloid magazine called *Nerve*, slapping O'Connor's face on the cover with that very headline.[6] McNeil enlisted a therapist to interpret statements she had made to the press as the supposed evidence, defending the move by telling *McCall's* that "people who get up on stage are severely damaged . . . we just want to see if the damage is interesting."[7]

So much for chivalry. In an attempt to stem the damage, both externally cast and self-inflicted, O'Connor wrote an open letter to the *Irish Times* in 1993 explaining how her childhood abuse had affected her life as a young adult who suddenly became famous and was famously ridiculed. She recognized that at times she had turned her grief inward, causing her to say and do things that were self-destructive. She pleaded for people to stop hurting her.[8]

O'Connor's hope in returning to Ireland was to make a private life for herself after more than a year of nonstop tumult. She rented a simple house in the Dublin suburbs right down the road from her sister Eimear. She made lunch dates with ex-husband John Reynolds. She enjoyed taking their six-year-old son Jake to school in the mornings and readying him for bed at night. She also started studying bel canto (singing from emotion) with Frank Merriman at the Parnell School of Music, telling a journalist from the *Guardian* that she believed singing lessons were the only therapy she needed.[9]

Before her record sales had ground to a halt, O'Connor had grossed at least a million dollars, enough to live comfortably without ever releasing another album. She had already announced that she was quitting the industry several times, once in 1990 and again in late 1992. But retirement wasn't in the cards, at least not yet.

Try as she might to be a "regular person," O'Connor kept writing new songs. She composed nearly all of the tracks for her next album in a single night, singing them into a tape recorder without input or criticism from her label, letting them flow from inside without suppressing her Irish accent for the first time in her career.

O'Connor would go on to describe *Universal Mother* as the most special album she had ever made.[10] Critics were not convinced. Writing for the *Baltimore Sun* in advance of the album's 1994 release, Matthew Gilbert refused to even listen to it. He dismissed O'Connor as a "fragile banshee," calling the public revelations about her childhood abuse "bitter."[11] He trivialized her reported suicide attempt, faulting her for being unable to bear the loathing of the fickle American public. Gilbert closed with the observation that she had grown her hair out just a bit, "softening her anti-look" as though it were nothing more than a cosmetic marketing gimmick.

In her review for *Rolling Stone*, Stephanie Zacharek took *Universal Mother* more seriously, giving it four stars, but she nevertheless criticized O'Connor for "telling us more about herself than we should probably know."[12] The Irish rock journalist Bill Graham was slightly more generous, calling the album "definitely the record of an artist determined to restart."[13]

It is true that the sound of this album was decidedly more commercial than O'Connor's show tunes, but *Universal*

Mother was still not a pop record, nor could it ever be one. What you hear is the work of excavation, swinging from emotion to emotion. Rage is what's most present in the hip-hop-inspired "Fire on Babylon" and "Red Football," a bid for reclamation of the female body. Tenderness comes into relief on "John, I Love You" which was written for her brother, and "My Darling Child," which was written for Jake. In "Am I a Human?" Jake also makes an adorable cameo, closing the circle between mother and child. The multitrack a cappella "All Babies" expresses hope for the future, with a reminder that we are all born of God and carry with us the potential to be divine.

What ties these songs together is that O'Connor is openly plumbing the depths of her childhood trauma while also addressing the complexity of her identity as a mother—not the typical fare of female pop artists in 1994. For example, Mariah Carey's "Hero" deployed clichés to encourage inner strength: "So when you feel like hope is gone / Look inside you and be strong." Celine Dion's "The Power of Love," relied on hackneyed platitudes: "Cause I'm your lady / And you are my man / Whenever you reach for me / I'll do all that I can." Ace of Base took the top spot on the charts with "The Sign," a cheerful reflection on the impending end of a relationship.

In contrast, the songs on *Universal Mother* suggest what O'Connor meant when she said singing was the only therapy she needed. The album's lead single, "Thank You for Hearing Me," was inspired by O'Connor's breakup with Gabriel, but it references their relationship only indirectly. Set to a pulse that is both ethereal and hypnotic, the lyrics appear to express gratitude. However, if you listen closely, especially toward the end, you'll hear a much more complicated nuance: "Thank you for breaking my heart / Thank you for tearing me apart / Now I have a strong, strong heart / Thank you for breaking my heart."

O'Connor also brings that quality of emotional honesty to her cover of Nirvana's "All Apologies," managing to best Kurt Cobain's version with a take that is even more intimate and devastating.[14] That said, the most brilliant and arresting song on the album is one you've probably never heard of: a Celtic rap called "Famine" that interpolates elements of "Tradition" from *Fiddler on the Roof* and the Beatles's "Eleanor Rigby" to draw parallels between O'Connor's experience as an abuse survivor and the experience of the Irish people who suffered during the Great Hunger.[15]

In the song, O'Connor attributes the Irish famine to patriarchal power structures and colonial oppression, showing how the innocence of the Irish was used as a trope and justification for abuse. She goes on to connect Ireland's historical experience to its ongoing struggles with child abuse, alcoholism, and drug addiction, comparing it to a battered child who's been driven out of their mind by traumatic experiences that have been disconnected from memories. She points out that breaking the cycle of abuse requires confronting the past, not simply denying or burying it:

> And if there ever is gonna be healing
> There has to be remembering and then grieving
> So that there then can be forgiving
> There has to be knowledge and understanding

In the '70s, John Lennon could pull off a song like "Mother." Bob Dylan could put out *Blood on the Tracks*, an entire album about the disintegration of his marriage

—and get away with claiming that the songs were really about characters in Chekhov's stories. But for a woman to make such a "personal" album like this even decades later, that was not going to fly.

Universal Mother would not push past the number thirty-six spot on *Billboard*'s US album chart. It sold only 217,000 copies, nearly 100,000 less than *Am I Not Your Girl?* and exponentially fewer units than *I Do Not Want What I Haven't Got.* The music videos for "Fire on Babylon" and "Famine" were both nominated for Grammy awards, but neither took the prize.

Maybe O'Connor anticipated this on some level. When she put out the record, she announced that she wouldn't be doing any press interviews to promote it; she planned to let the songs speak for themselves. She nevertheless agreed to an interview about "Famine" with *Irish Times* columnist John Waters, who at least wanted to engage with her on an intellectual level.

Waters had recently published *Race of Angels: Ireland and the Genesis of U2*, which used biography, cultural history, and memoir to argue that U2's music reflected something akin to an "Irish mind" informed by the Great Hunger and its aftermath. Waters, saw a similar postcolonial worldview in O'Connor's "Famine."

Although he was interested in her ideas, he also pursued O'Connor romantically. At the time, she had recently ended a relationship and suffered a miscarriage. She wanted another baby, but not necessarily a husband. They became involved and she got pregnant, but they parted ways when O'Connor was only eight weeks along in her pregnancy. She moved back to England, and was on the bill for the 1995 Lollapalooza tour, but she had to leave early due to pregnancy complications. Her daughter Roisin was born in March 1996. The co-parenting arrangement she had with Waters called for Roisin to be raised by O'Connor in London, while Waters would be her legal guardian in Ireland.

Despite disappointing sales of *Universal Mother*, O'Connor's career was far from over. In addition to appearing in Neil Jordan's 1997 film *The Butcher Boy*, where she was cast as a foul-mouthed Virgin Mary, O'Connor released two more records that year. The first was a "best of" compilation, an effort on the part of Chrysalis to eke the value from her back catalog before she jumped ship for a new worldwide four-album deal with Atlantic Records, worth a reported $8 million.[16] The second was *Gospel Oak*, an EP of songs about forgiveness and hope, dedicated to "the people of Israel, Rwanda, and Northern Ireland."

Named for the northwest London neighborhood where O'Connor lived and saw a therapist six days a week, *Gospel Oak* featured political songs such as "Petit Poulet," a response to the Rwandan genocide, and "This Is a Rebel Song," a put-down of U2 for claiming that "Sunday Bloody Sunday" *wasn't* a rebel song. It was also informed by her experiences as a trauma survivor, reflected in self-affirming songs such as "This is to Mother You" and "I am Enough for Myself."

Like her previous post-1990 efforts, it stiffed, selling a mere 70,000 copies. However, O'Connor was invited to perform as part of the lineup for the 1998 Lilith Fair, and she also started collaborating with Beck, members of the Smashing Pumpkins, and other A-list indie artists in a short-lived supergroup called Ashtar Command. Though her quiet engagement to TV ad composer John Robertson was also short-lived, at least the gossip rags laid off.

Whenever O'Connor did speak to reporters, it always

seemed to come back to the same old questions: *Did you really mean to tear up the photo of the pope? Do you regret boycotting the Grammys? How did it feel to be booed off the stage at the Dylan show? Would you go back and do it all again if you could?*[17]

O'Connor held her own, pushing back against the way the media treated her, calling out the complicity of journalists in provoking some of her most outrageous and outrage-provoking behavior, but privately she was facing a new set of challenges.

Waters, like O'Connor's father, had become a leading advocate for the rights of men seeking contact with their children following divorce or separation. But he wasn't satisfied with the shared custody arrangement he made with O'Connor. He filed multiple anonymous complaints with the London police accusing O'Connor of neglecting their daughter. The social services agency found no evidence to support the allegations and, in a rare move, even went so far as putting out a public statement that it was dropping its investigation because they found Roisin to be "very happy and loved."

Despite the public validation, O'Connor's mental state deteriorated under the sustained pressure of the accusations and relentless scrutiny. After another widely reported suicide attempt, she feared that she would lose a court battle over custody, and she told friends that Waters scared her into temporarily giving it up—on Mother's Day no less.[18]

O'Connor stopped eating and dropped to less than a hundred pounds and was hospitalized. When she was released, it was reported in the tabloids that she visited Waters's Dublin home, telling him that she intended to take her daughter out for a walk. Instead, she and three-year-old Roisin boarded a plane back to London, where O'Connor's home had been outfitted with a surveillance system and round-the-clock guards.[19] Details of their ultimate custody resolution were never made public per a 1999 court order.

Shortly thereafter O'Connor shocked the world again, appearing as a guest on Ireland's RTÉ *Late Late Show*, where she told host Gay Byrne that if she had not become a musician, her ambition would have been to become a priest.[20] Wearing clerical clothing, O'Connor explained that she had connected with Michael Cox, a bishop in the Traditionalist Catholic "Tridentine" movement, a break-away group not affiliated with or recognized by the mainstream Catholic Church.

After six weeks of theological study, Cox had ordained her as Mother Bernadette Marie in a hotel room in Lourdes. She claimed the authority to perform Mass, baptize children, and administer last rites. As her first act of charity, O'Connor donated money to set up a shelter and healing center for Ireland's nomadic ethnic minority group known as the traveling community.

Refusing to see her callings as incompatible, O'Connor also returned to making music, embarking on her first full studio album in six years with the help of high-profile producers, including Eurythmics's Dave Stewart as well as Brian Eno, Adrian Sherwood, and Wyclef Jean. When she set out to promote the album in 2000, she wore her priestly garments, a crucifix, and a clerical collar.[21] She called the new work *Faith and Courage*, a collection of eclectic songs about forgiveness and redemption, and a reflection of the realization that she needed both to survive.

"I have done many things / To give you reason not to listen to me," O'Connor sings on the track "The Lamb's Book of Life." But she reminded the public *why they should listen* in "No Man's Woman," a fierce cry for female independence. In "What Doesn't Belong to Me," she sings, "Take back the shame you gave me / Take back the anger you gave me / Take back the hatred you gave me for me / Take back the anger that nearly killed me / Take back what doesn't belong to me." The closing track, "Kyrié Eléison," put a mischievous Rasta spin on the first section of the Catholic mass.

Faith and Courage performed comparatively well, selling more than 200,000 copies in the United States alone, with "No Man's Woman" even spawning a Top 40 single. To promote it, O'Connor went all out on the press circuit, appearing confident and relaxed in interviews on *The Tonight Show* and Queen Latifah's talk show, where she shaved a fan's head before a live studio audience before rapping along with the host.[22]

But it was a promotional interview with *Curve Magazine* that made the biggest headlines. In response to the interviewer's question about why she had such a significant following among lesbians, O'Connor replied, "Although I haven't been very open about that and throughout most of my life I've gone out with blokes because I haven't necessarily been terribly comfortable about being a lesbian. But I actually am a lesbian."[23]

What did lesbians make of this revelation? In my recollection, not a lot. For one thing, the annals of rock were not lacking for queer women, or women thought to be queer, from Janis Joplin and Dusty Springfield to Joan Jett and Jane Wiedlin. For another, in part as an outgrowth of

1990s activism in the wake of the HIV/AIDS crisis, queer visibility had begun to soar. No longer willing to be erased or pushed to the margins, women-loving-women were suddenly busting out of the closet, splinters flying in all directions.

Madonna got the ball rolling in 1991 when she told *The Advocate*, "I think everybody has a bisexual nature. That's my theory. I could be wrong." But it officially kicked off in 1992 when, to virtually no one's surprise, k.d. lang came out. Then it was Melissa Etheridge in 1993.

Not to be upstaged, in 1994 Madonna and Sandra Bernhard coyly name-checked New York City lesbian bars like Meow Mix, Cubbyhole, the Clit Club, and Henrietta Hudson, and were very good at being photographed there. Whether they were actually lovers, and/or both or either also involved with OG gal pal Ingrid Casares, was kind of moot.[24]

That's because Sophie B. Hawkins, who identified as "omnisexual," had already taken the codependent lesbian rescue anthem "Damn I Wish I Was Your Lover" to number five on the Billboard Hot 100 in 1992. The video for the song was deemed "too erotic" and therefore banned by MTV, although an edit eventually made it over the line. You can find a different video of Hawkins and Melissa Etheridge performing it as a live and hilariously awkward duet on VH-1 in 1995, the same year that Jill Sobule cracked the Top 40 when she matter-of-factly proclaimed "I Kissed a Girl." And by the way, she liked it.

Within the space of just a few years, having a girl crush became normcore. "Lipstick lesbians" were the subject of seemingly endless fascination, spilling over into every aspect of pop culture. For their staged "showmance," a lingerie-clad Cindy Crawford gave k.d. lang a suggestive shave on the cover of *Vanity Fair* (1993). In real life, Ellen DeGeneres came out (1994), as did Anne Heche (albeit briefly, from 1997 to 2000).

Women started falling in love with each other, or at least hooking up, in films such as *Poison Ivy* (1992), *Go Fish* (1994), *The Incredibly True Adventures of Two Girls in Love* (1995), *Boys on the Side* (1995), *Bound* (1996), *Chasing Amy* (1997), *Wild Things* (1998), and *High Art* (1998). In the TV world, Ross had to negotiate child custody with his lesbian ex-wife Carol on *Friends* (starting in 1994).

If some straight people thought that O'Connor's shaved head, or her "antipatriarchal" fury, made her "look" like a lesbian, they were missing a lot. Lesbians were no longer exclusively stereotyped as the labrys-wielding, overalls-donning, Mary Daly–worshipping dykes of yesteryear. In the 1990s, we also wore our queerness ironically—perhaps an oversized rugby or flannel shirt over a T-shirt or tied around the waist of men's Levis, or black Doc Martens, a Perfecto jacket over a muscle shirt, and at least one body piercing and an undercut. You could present as cis and straight and be 100 percent gay—or present as butch as fuck and still be straight.

To us there was nothing shocking about O'Connor's revelation—except that it wasn't exactly true, and that was going to be a problem. Just as the straight public was reeling from what she said, within the space of two weeks O'Connor dialed back her statement, telling a reporter from the *Independent*, "I believe it was overcompensating of me to declare myself a lesbian. It was not a publicity stunt. I was trying to make someone else feel better. And have subsequently caused pain for myself. I am not in a box of any description."[25]

"I am not in a box of any description" might seem like a perfectly reasonable statement; in fact, for many today, it's the very definition of queer. But who exactly was she trying to make feel better by calling herself a lesbian? And why, in the millisecond in between her coming out and her clarification, had O'Connor accepted an invitation to co-headline the world's first "openly gay" touring music festival?

Whereas Lollapalooza took its name from the term for "extraordinarily impressive," *Wotapalava*, organized by the Pet Shop Boys, was meant as a wink to the British slang expression "What a palaver," meaning "What a fuss over nothing." The eighteen-city 2001 tour was to feature O'Connor, along with other gay artists, including Soft Cell, Rufus Wainwright, the Magnetic Fields, and DJs Junior Vasquez and Danny Tenaglia.

However, five hours before a major news conference to announce the event, O'Connor sent a fax to organizers saying she would have to pull out of the lineup due to "unforeseeable family circumstances." After a brief scramble to replace her with the straight but gay-friendly Grace Jones, promoters announced that they planned instead to postpone the tour for a year, leading some to speculate that tepid ticket sales made proceeding untenable. To Neil Tennant, who was said to have been the driving force behind *Wotapalava*, this turn of events should not have come as a surprise.

In 1997 Lilith Fair raked in $16 million gross in its first year—the top earner of any touring festival. In its first three years it generated more than $10 million for charity, with a dollar from every ticket going to causes such as the Breast Cancer Fund; the Rape, Abuse & Incest National Network; AIDS research and awareness organization

LIFEbeat; and Planned Parenthood, which had booths in the Village area during each Lilith Fair show.[26]

Like Lilith Fair, *Wotapalava* was supposed to be about the music, not explicitly the politics. But Lilith's touring roster was much bigger, and it was anchored by an all-star lineup including Sarah McLachlan, Sheryl Crowe, and Tracy Chapman, all of whom were at the height of their commercial success. In contrast, aside from the Pet Shop Boys and O'Connor, *Wotapalava*'s bill largely comprised critical darlings who had not yet achieved broad recognition, or in the case of Soft Cell, were considered past their prime. But perhaps *Wotapalava*'s biggest failure was the organizer's inability to see that Lilith's audiences came out to see music made by women — not necessarily women's music. In fact, 30 percent to 40 percent of the audience was male.

Gay, like women, is not a musical genre. It was a hard sell to suggest that the artists' gay sexuality was a fuss about nothing, yet use it as a selling point for a touring festival that was presumably meant to attract a broad audience.

Aside from what she said in her fax, O'Connor never spoke about why she said yes to headlining the tour or why she then pulled out. Maybe she said yes because she was looking for her next move, having quietly shed her priestly frocks and, amid a corporate restructuring, parted ways with Atlantic.[27] Maybe she wanted to be an "ally" to the gay community. But one thing is for sure: it would not have been a good look for her to marry a man, Nick Sommerlad, two months into the "gay" tour. That's what she did, and *Wotapalava* never happened.

O'Connor jumped back into music again with the 2002 release of *Sean-Nós Nua*, a new twist on traditional Irish folk songs, produced by the folk artist Dónal Lunny. She sat for as many promotional interviews as she could, but much of the buzz centered on reviving the *SNL* scandal, and her cover of the Canadian folk song "Peggy Gordon," which O'Connor had reinterpreted as a lesbian anthem by virtue of maintaining the first-person perspective. When she sang of her darling, Peggy, "I am so deeply in love that I can't deny it." It sure sounded like a coming-out statement, or, worse, like queerbaiting.

Perhaps to avoid further hot water with lesbians and her new husband, O'Connor wrote in the liner notes that she approached the song from the lesbian point of view rather than from her own lesbian standpoint, framing it as an expression of affirmation rather than identification.

"It is usually sung by men in Ireland but I like it as a song sung by a female. I first heard it from a woman who was singing it as an expression of mourning for the loss of her female lover," O'Connor explained in the notes. "I fell in love with the song as an expression of homosexual love, which often is not allowed [to] voice itself in Ireland. It is a whisper of a song which to me expresses the sheer fragility of homosexual love in a world that teaches, against God, that love is conditional."

Although *Sean-Nós Nua* went to number one in Ireland, it remained largely unnoticed by the rest of the world. *Uncut* ungenerously slammed it, calling the album "a sentimental indulgence destined for a theme-pub half-life."[28]

The timing of its release, almost to the day a decade after *SNL* — went virtually unnoticed. Jake Tapper, then a writer for *Salon*, was one of the only journalists to use the moment to publicly acknowledge that O'Connor had been correct about the Catholic Church's child abuse scandal.

Even so, he hedged, going out of his way to mention that O'Connor had explained to him, as she had to journalists many times before, that she meant only to rip up a symbol of the Church and not to attack the man or the faith. Tapper further tried to help by mentioning that O'Connor didn't think anyone who was offended by her actions owed *her* an apology. He sidestepped completely the question of whether anyone owed an apology to her.[29]

Perhaps by 2002 O'Connor had already made too many public statements that came across as gaffes, nonsense, or stunts. If you didn't think of her as a kook, she was at best an imperfect witness, someone who was all too easily written off. Credit for exposing the Church's abuse scandal went elsewhere, primarily to a series of articles in the *Boston Globe* in 2002 that led to hundreds of criminal cases and a sea change in public opinion, not to mention Pulitzers for the investigative team.

Rather than looking back to *SNL* as the end of her career, O'Connor kept flirting with the idea of returning to pop music, even recording a few songs with Massive Attack in 2003. She was set to open for the band on a leg of its European tour, but she pulled out, citing health issues.

She followed by putting out an unannounced double album of live, unreleased, and demo recordings entitled *She Who Dwells in the Secret Place of the Most High Shall Abide Under the Shadow of the Almighty*, but then took another about-face, abruptly announcing on her website that she'd had enough of the music business. In a farewell note posted on her website, she pled with her fans for understanding:

So I ask with love, that I be left in peace and privacy by people who love my records. My advise [*sic*] to anyone who ever admires a so-called celebrity if u see them in the street, don't even look at them. If u love them, then the lovingest thing u can do to show them so is leave them alone and don't stare at them! . . . Or make them get their picture taken, or write their names on bits of paper. That's pieces of them. And one day they wake up with nothing left of themselves to give.

O'Connor had quit the music business multiple times before, for example, in 1992, after the Bob Dylan tribute concert, and very briefly in 1999, after she was ordained. But she needed to keep singing, so, like her previous resignations, this one didn't last long. In fact, 2003 shaped up to be one of her busiest years yet. After the release of a concert and documentary DVD spanning the course of her career called *Goodnight, Thank You. You've Been a Lovely Audience*, she appeared on a Dolly Parton tribute album, singing the song "Dagger Through the Heart," as well as collaborating with the Irish accordionist Sharon Shannon.

When O'Connor spoke to the press, she tried in vain to clarify her previous statements about her sexuality, telling RTÉ that although most of her past relationships were with men, she had also been in three relationships with women. She then split with Sommerlad, but not for a woman. In 2004 she gave birth to her third child, Shane, who was conceived with *Sean-Nós Nua* producer Dónal Lunny. At the time, Lunny had been married to his second wife for only two years, and they had a baby only six months before Shane's birth.

O'Connor continued making music—releasing two albums in 2005. The first was *Collaborations*, a compilation of past appearances with artists including U2 and Peter Gabriel. The second was the Sly and Robbie-produced reggae-roots cover album *Throw Down Your Arms*, which was recorded in Bob Marley's studio in Jamaica and included a new recording of "War" with Marley's original lyrics restored.

O'Connor tried to explain her heartfelt connection to this music, telling NPR's Debbie Elliot, "You know, there are huge blood ties, for a start. You know, there are huge ties between Africa and Ireland going way back, you know, before Jamaica even existed as it is now. And we were colonized by the same people and by the same religion in a lot of ways. And we have the same, I think, similarities in our music in that there's a huge kind of longing, yearning, and calling in the music from Ireland and Jamaica, particularly the singing."[30]

But her Jamaican roots music was an even harder sell than her Irish album, and as with that venture, most of the public's attention was focused on her personal life. Paparazzi caught a shot of O'Connor with American businessman Frank Bonadio, who was in the process of leaving his wife, the renowned Irish singer Mary Coughlan. A string of leaked X-rated text messages confirmed the alleged affair, and a pregnant O'Connor moved into the house Bonadio and his wife had shared. In December 2006, O'Connor gave birth to her fourth child, Yeshua, but a series of public fights between Coughlan and O'Connor led O'Connor to break up with Bonadio two months later.

In June 2007, O'Connor released *Theology*, another self-funded collection of Rastafari-inspired spiritual songs.

When she sat for a promotional interview with the *London Mirror*, however, scant attention was paid to the music or the business model. Again, coverage was a recap of all of her past scandals, leading with O'Connor's renewal of her accusations against Prince, even though she had previously disclaimed them in a 2003 interview where she had told Graham Norton that Prince was "a sweet guy" and rumors of her assault were "much exaggerated by the press."[31] Although *Theology* managed to chart in Ireland, its peak position on the UK Album Chart was only 157 and its first-week US sales fell short of five thousand units.

If you're exhausted and depressed by what I've just told you about O'Connor's life post-1992, imagine what it must have been like to live it on repeat. As *Guardian* columnist Suzanne Moore once observed, it was impossible to name another woman who could generate the kind of publicity O'Connor did over the years without taking her clothes off. But it was never the good kind of publicity, the kind that would have helped her to revive and sustain a musical career on her own terms. Fifteen years after *SNL*, O'Connor was selling lots of newspapers, but not records.

WRECKING BALL

Perhaps O'Connor could have done more to pursue a publicity-free existence, forgoing attempts at musical comebacks to work on the goal of healing. Over time, the public would have lost interest in her and moved on to other celebrities. But in a way, that was the problem.

Self-imposed obscurity would have been difficult for someone like O'Connor, who was dependent on others for a sense of who she was, whose self-image had been so deformed, first by her family, and then by the culture. So she found herself in an endless cycle of doing things to get attention, then taking in the negative reaction, then wanting to be left alone, then feeling like being left alone meant she didn't exist.

I think this goes a long way toward explaining O'Connor's 2007 decision to appear as a guest on *Oprah*, where she acknowledged for the first time that she was suffering from bipolar disorder, a diagnosis that had been made four years earlier, right around the time she pulled out of the tour with Massive Attack and announced that she was quitting the music business.

"It's like being a bucket with holes in it," she told Oprah and her audience of five million viewers. "Just leaking tears from every pore." O'Connor theorized that the violence she had experienced as a child, plus the pressures of fame and the way she had been treated by the media over the years, all contributed to the deterioration of her mental health.

"I started making records and suddenly became this pop star thing, but I never had time to form my own identity, if you like, or recover from my upbringing," she told Oprah. "It really confused me. I didn't know who I was or what I was. And I didn't have anybody around me who I knew before, so you're not seeing yourself reflected back at yourself from anyone around you. It can be a massive identity crisis." She went on to express sympathy for younger pop stars, such as Britney Spears, whom she saw going through some of the same things.

Superficially, O'Connor and Spears were nothing alike. But Spears had also became a pop superstar at a young age, signing her first recording contract at fifteen. At eighteen, Spears's 1999 debut album, . . . *Baby One More Time*, went double platinum, selling more than 30 million copies worldwide. One year later, her follow up, *Oops! . . . I Did it Again*, sold over a million copies upon its release.

Spears's monumental commercial success afforded her the opportunity to take creative control, writing and co-producing more of her own material, much like O'Connor. But like O'Connor, Spears still struggled to be taken seriously as an artist, and the turbulence in her private life often played out in public.

In 2004, Spears's fifty-five-hour marriage to childhood friend Jason Allen Alexander was annulled when a court petition stated that she "lacked understanding of her actions." Her second marriage, to Kevin Federline, a backup dancer she'd known for only a few months, came at a time when he had just terminated a relationship with another woman, with whom he was expecting his second child. His whirlwind romance with Spears and its dissolution were chronicled in real time in a UPN reality show aptly titled *Britney and Kevin: Chaotic*.

In early 2006, Spears was photographed driving with her young son on her lap, a lapse in judgment she attributed to an argument with a paparazzo. She was said to have repeatedly flashed her naked crotch at another photographer on a different occasion and was photographed several times appearing disheveled, fueling rumors of drinking and substance abuse.

Two months after the birth of her second son, Spears filed for divorce from Federline. Then her aunt, with whom she had a close relationship, died from ovarian cancer. Spears checked into a rehab clinic in Antigua in January 2007, but she only lasted a day before returning to California, to ex-husband Kevin Federline's home, where she demanded to see their kids.

When Federline refused, Spears walked into a hair salon complaining that her hair extensions were too tight and asked the stylist to shave her head. When the stylist refused, Spears took the clippers into her own hands. Two bodyguards were there to ensure that there were no paparazzi watching, but as her flowing locks fell to the floor, photographers appeared as though on cue, frantically snapping photos that went public immediately. When Spears then headed to a nearby tattoo parlor, more paparazzi were camped out to document the inking of a small cross on her hip and dainty pair of lips on her wrist.

Was this a defiant bid for independence? A desperate cry for help? Would legions of young girls suddenly follow suit? It's strange to look back and try to make sense of all the media hysteria over Spears's "bizarre" behavior. Then again, they'd seen a bald, tattooed woman before, and they knew that meant trouble.

When O'Connor spoke of Spears on Oprah in October of that year, she couldn't have known that Spears's mental health was really deteriorating, or that in January 2008, Dr. Phil, whose license had lapsed two years earlier, would reach out to Spears when she was being treated in the psychiatric unit at Cedars-Sinai Medical Center to pitch her on the idea of appearing on his show.[1]

O'Connor could not have anticipated that Dr. Phil would try to justify his actions by claiming that he approached Spears at the request of her family, who he claimed were on board with the idea of appearing with her as part of a "family intervention." Nor could she have known that Spears would soon be placed in a conservatorship that would remain in place for the next thirteen years. But O'Connor certainly related to Spears—not just as a woman or a woman in music, but as a woman in music whose private turmoil was being played out publicly and exploited by others.

Although some lauded O'Connor for her openness about her own situation, which they saw as a major milestone in creating a space for public discourse around mental health, others saw it as yet another bid for attention. This was, after all, Oprah's couch—and not the couch of a private therapist.

And there was another problem: O'Connor had said many of these things many times before over the years, which led to sympathy fatigue, even among her most loyal fans. They would hear her go on to say that she'd been misdiagnosed as bipolar, that she had been suffering from borderline personality disorder and/or posttraumatic stress disorder, fibromyalgia, agoraphobia, endometriosis, kidney stones, and other various ailments. When she expressed the desire to be left alone, it seemed disingenuous, or at least contradictory to many of her statements and actions.

Rather than dialing down her public profile, O'Connor reunited with old manager Fachtna O'Ceallaigh in 2008 and managed to stay out of the headlines only briefly until she got married again, this time to long-time musical collaborator Steve Cooney in 2010—a marriage that lasted less than a year.

O'Connor rebounded by writing a series of columns for Ireland's *Independent*, in which she spoke in frank terms about being "desperate for sex" and detailing her specific sexual wants and needs, telling readers that "inanimate objects are starting to look good."[2] She also posted these writings on her website, for all the world to see, drawing immediate rebuke.

That response only motivated her to continue writing, explaining that the more she scandalized people, the funnier her "inner child" found it. I think that says a lot about what was driving her posts: the conflict between her wounded self and the self who knew that establishing boundaries would have helped shield her from criticism.

The other tricky thing was that her "want ads" appeared to work. They brought her a slew of new Twitter followers, including a drug counselor, Barry Herridge, whom she married in Las Vegas on her forty-fifth birthday, only weeks after they first met.

From the get-go, this fourth marriage appeared doomed, starting with the fact that the chosen venue was the Little

White Wedding Chapel, the same place where Britney Spears had wed Jason Allen Alexander.[3] There were also unconfirmed reports of a wedding night search for marijuana that ended in a crack cocaine purchase. O'Connor's continuous reporting of the day's proceedings was posted on her website:

> Dear friends . . . amongst whom I include whomever may be reading this with a view to writing about the glorious marriage. Am blogging this cus media people are naturally seeking me. On sunday I will put up blog on whole day. Too glorious for words. For now though, as you will appreciate, It's a bit of a 'Can't. Talk. Cock. In. Mouth'. Situation.

The couple split up days later, reconciled, then split again, all within the space of a few short weeks. In between, O'Connor tweeted and blogged, posted photos, and occasionally called in to radio stations and spoke with reporters. It may have seemed like performance art, but it wasn't. A few weeks later, O'Connor boarded a flight to the United States to perform at the Golden Globes with some pills in her bag—and a plan to intentionally overdose. She instead checked into a psychiatric facility and promised to stay away from social media and the news.

O'Connor's ongoing search for love, and attention, inspired her next album, 2012's *How About I Be Me (And You Be You)?* On the title track, O'Connor pleads with those who scorned her, "Don't stop me talking about love / How am I going to find out what I'm dreaming of." A raw, riveting cover of John Grant's "Queen of Denmark" showed that she still knew how to own a song: "I wanted to change the world / But I could not even change my underwear / And when the shit got really, really out of hand / I had it all the way up to my hairline."

O'Connor took a pointed jab at Bono and other Irish artists who value celebrity culture and materialism in "V.I.P.," reminding them that higher values should prevail. But alongside that familiar theme was a song about addiction of all kinds, "Reason with Me," and the tender love song "The Wolf is Getting Married," which glows with these simple but beautiful lines: "Your smile makes me smile / Your laugh makes me laugh / Your joy gives me joy / Your hope gives me hope."

Will Hermes of *Rolling Stone* praised O'Connor's empathy and wit.[4] Dave Simpson of the *Guardian* even liked the tracks with bite, remarking that "it's thrilling to hear such vitriol and indignation, qualities in short supply in current pop."[5] Although How *About I Be Me (And You Be You)?* sold a disappointing 18,000 copies, a tour was in the works to boost its performance.

The wrinkle was O'Connor's recent weight gain, a side effect of medication she had been prescribed to treat bipolar disorder, which generated tabloid headlines such as the *Daily Mail's* "Sinéad O'Connor Is Unrecognizable as She Dons Unflattering Stomach-Baring Outfit for Irish Performance."[6] To shed the pounds quickly, O'Connor abruptly discontinued the medication and suffered a mental health crisis. After she attempted suicide, she reached out on Twitter to tell fans that she was in danger and to ask for psychiatric help.

A different medicine prescribed to treat her symptoms only amplified her suicidal thoughts, forcing O'Connor to cancel her tour dates. She returned home, exhausted and facing an onslaught of legal problems from the cancellation. O'Connor left too many details in O'Ceallaigh's hands—although she was uncharacteristically careful about how she described matters in the press, O'Connor said that a forensic accountant had uncovered business dealings of which she had neither knowledge nor consent.

O'Connor credited her first husband and longtime collaborator, John Reynolds, for helping her get out of the hole. Having produced or co-produced several of her previous albums, Reynolds encouraged her to begin working on her next album as a way to regain control of her life, music, and image.

O'Connor began listening to Chicago bluesmen such as Buddy Guy, Magic Sam, and Howlin' Wolf. Then Reynolds brought her some brief melodies, which she filled in and paired with lyrics, letting the music convey the emotion, using simple and direct language to convey her ideas.

On "Take Me to Church," O'Connor sings, "I don't want to cry no more / I don't want to die no more." On "Kisses Like Mine," she addresses the cyclic troubles in her romantic life: "See, I'm special forces / They call me in after divorces," then a bit later allows that "I'm just not the keeping kind." In "Eight Good Reasons," she acknowledges, "You know I'm not from this place / I'm from a different time, different space."

These songs amounted to O'Connor's strongest and most direct statement of unconditional self-acceptance yet, the moment where she finally began to own the "Sinéad is crazy" narrative rather than trying to explain herself. "I don't do embarrassment" became much more than a nice tagline to spin in interviews. It became something closer to a true statement.

The album's title, *I'm Not Bossy, I'm the Boss*, came to

O'Connor after she'd heard then Facebook COO Sheryl Sandberg claim that branding girls and women as "bossy" discourages them from vying for leadership positions and should therefore be banned. Seeing a parallel in the music industry, O'Connor thought women should push back against self-censorship and reclaim the word "bossy."

To signify that she was unwilling to limit her own creative self-expression, the cover art for the album featured a newly slender O'Connor in a way we had never seen her before. In her late forties, she was clad in a tight black latex dress, high heels, a long black wig, and makeup. She was saying to the world, "I'm in charge. I decide how to represent myself."

The album's 2014 release did cause a splash, particularly on the heels of a nasty public feud with Miley Cyrus. In 2013, the 20-year-old singer had released a video directed by sleaze king Terry Richardson for her single "Wrecking Ball." An obvious rip-off of the video for "Nothing Compares 2 U," it framed Cyrus in extreme close-up with her hair shorn. Although she sings of heartbreak, Cyrus won't be defeated by it. She sheds a tear and her clothing, suggestively licking a sledgehammer and straddling a wrecking ball.

To promote the song and her accompanying album, *Bangerz*, Cyrus appeared on the cover of *Rolling Stone*, posing nude by a pool with her short hair slicked back, her makeup smudged, and her tongue licking her shoulder suggestively. In an interview with contributing editor Josh Eells, Cyrus spoke about shedding her good-girl Hannah Montana image and coming into her own identity, which amounted to buying a pair of Doc Martens boots and shaving her head.[7]

"I need my own *Rolling Stone* column where every issue it's just something crazy I do," Cyrus told Eells. Four days before their interview Cyrus had pulled off a major publicity stunt involving Robin Thicke and a foam finger at the MTV Video Music Awards, a performance she described to Eells as "toned down" for television. To commemorate her *Rolling Stone* cover, Cyrus took him along to get real-time tattoos on both her feet. One said "Rolling" and the other, "$tone."

Cyrus acknowledged that the "Wrecking Ball" video was an homage to O'Connor's video for "Nothing Compares 2 U" and identified O'Connor as a personal inspiration. Cyrus claimed that the tear she shed in the video was as real as O'Connor's, though inspired by the recent death of her dog. Depending on whom you asked, Cyrus came across as an idiot — or, like Madonna, a genius who knew exactly what to say to generate buzz.

Several media outlets approached O'Connor for comment, but she chose to respond in an open letter, one of the many she'd written over the course of her career. Although Cyrus was antithetical to everything she stood for, O'Connor saw in the twenty-year-old a version of her younger self — a woman who was trying to make it in a misogynistic industry that valued women only for their sex appeal. She also thought of Cyrus's young fans, future generations of women and girls who would be groomed to see themselves in these terms.[8]

In her letter, O'Connor expressed concern for Cyrus, encouraging her to realize that she was more than her body. O'Connor implored her not to let herself "be pimped" by the industry, closing by advising Cyrus to "kindly fire any motherfucker who hasn't expressed alarm, because they don't care about you." But rather than seeing O'Connor's letter as an expression of sincere, almost maternal, concern, Cyrus took it as a slam and promptly retaliated on Twitter, where she reposted several anguished Tweets that O'Connor had written two years earlier about her failed marriage to Herridge and her search for a psychiatrist. Cyrus's cruel caption was "Before there was Amanda Bynes . . . There was . . ."

Bynes, like Cyrus, was a former child star. Like O'Connor, she had publicly identified herself as a survivor of childhood abuse and spoke openly about her struggles with mental health. Cyrus's mocking of both women enraged O'Connor, who threatened to take legal action. She penned a second letter to Cyrus, this time calling her "anti-female" and "f–king" stupid," to which Cyrus replied by tweeting that she didn't have time to write back because she was hosting and performing on *SNL* later that week.

Cyrus closed her tweet by saying, "So if youd like to meet up and talk lemme know in your next letter. ;)" Unfortunately, O'Connor remained engaged, telling Cyrus in a third letter that she had no interest in meeting her but demanded an apology for her abusive remarks, concluding, "When you end up in the psych ward or rehab I'll be happy to visit you . . . and would not lower myself to mock you."

Cyrus then brought the beef to the *Today Show*, where a pre-disgraced Matt Lauer asked her whether she was surprised by the attention.[9] "Not really," Cyrus responded. "I'm an artist, so I'm hoping I get a little attention. Otherwise, my record sales might be a little sketch." Lauer asked whether she had any regrets, anything she'd like to do over. When Cyrus said no, he dug in, bringing up O'Connor, whom he described as one of her critics. Cyrus praised O'Connor as an artist and songwriter, reiterated that the "Wrecking Ball" video was inspired by her, then expressed faux dismay over O'Connor's reaction, describing it as being akin to someone saying they respected you and your reply was "you suck."

"That was kind of crazy," Cyrus told Lauer with a coy smile, "but I'm a big fan of hers so it doesn't really matter." Cyrus went on to brag about how the true measure of her character is how she treats people, and that people know that she's a good person.

That triggered a fourth letter from O'Connor, which slammed Cyrus for not seeming to grasp the mental health implications of her mockery.[10] O'Connor pointed out that Cyrus's comments prompted people to write to Sineád urging her to commit suicide. O'Connor called on Cyrus to apologize again, emphasizing that it was a way to set things right. Of course, Cyrus did nothing of the sort.

Singer-songwriter and performance artist Amanda Palmer jumped into the spectacle with her own unsolicited open letter to O'Connor, whom she also praised as a personal inspiration, but argued that since Cyrus was "writing the plot and signing the checks," she, rather than the industry, was in control. Although Palmer acknowledged the difficulty of achieving control in a male-dominated and often misogynistic industry, she concluded her letter by soliciting O'Connor to "give our young women the right weapons to fight with as they charge naked into battle, instead of ordering them to get back in the house and put some goddamn clothes on."

What on earth could those right weapons possibly be?

Certainly not more foam fingers or fodder for the Twitter-sphere, which is what the exchange metastasized into: more letters and then think pieces about the letters, all ultimately a circular firing squad. O'Connor had intended not to chastise Cyrus, but to advocate for her. Palmer had intended not to chastise O'Connor, but to advocate for women. In the end, nothing changed. Cyrus kept twerking. O'Connor kept warning. One kept selling records. The other not so much.

THINGS NEED TO CHANGE

My point is not to defend everything O'Connor has ever said or done, but to ask what she did to provoke so much contempt, mockery, and dismissal — aside from destroying a photo of the pope thirty years ago. And aside from doing something we all now know was intended to sound the alarm about something that was actually happening and, in fact, evil. And aside from something that in 2013 would bring Alex Gibney six primetime Emmy Awards and a Peabody, and in 2015 would bring Tom McCarthy two Academy Awards for *Spotlight*, a dramatization of the *Boston Globe* investigation that was credited with breaking the Catholic Church's child abuse scandal in the United States.

Was it O'Connor's ever-evolving religious beliefs? The Beatles, Bob Dylan, Leonard Cohen, Lou Reed, Cat Stevens, Alice Cooper, and Jermaine Jackson were just a few of the other musicians who explored, deepened, or changed their faiths, often more than once, without garnering disdain. Prince once even told talk show host Tavis Smiley that his childhood epilepsy had literally been cured by an angel.[1]

Was it O'Connor's queer, perhaps undefinable, sexuality? David Bowie, Lou Reed, Iggy Pop, Elton John, Pete Townshend, and Kurt Cobain publicly acknowledged their attraction for and/or sexual relationships with men, even though every single one was married to at least one woman, often more.

Was it O'Connor's out-of-wedlock children, born out of relationships with different partners? Not a problem for Bob Dylan, Mick Jagger, Rod Stewart, Willie Nelson, Ray Charles, or Bob Marley, each of whom had many more kids than she did and were widely regarded as studs, not sluts.

Was it O'Connor's struggles with mental health, which were often lived out loud? Brian Wilson, Ray Davies, Nick Drake, Syd Barrett, and Kurt Cobain weren't written off for their diagnoses. On the contrary, their quirks and sensitivities were often portrayed as a side effect or even the cause of their genius.

What's different about O'Connor isn't just that she acknowledged or sought attention for her transgressions, or even that she was a woman. It's that she held up a mirror to society, exposing its gaslighting, hypocrisy, and double standards with respect to gender, race, and the economic drivers of the music industry.

Even if she were crazy, O'Connor showed us that we were crazy-making. When the industry and its messaging arm, the media, didn't like what she revealed in that reflection, they tried to smash her. We as a society went along with it to avoid seeing how it smashed us, too. Consider that over all of these years, not a single public figure who attacked her has since apologized, not one has acknowledged that she was correct about anything, and very few public figures have consistently defended her—including women.

Denying that she was mistreated and distancing ourselves from the wreckage didn't work in the long run. Women who tried to play by the music industry's rules still experienced costly trade-offs. Consider Whitney Houston. Recent posthumous documentaries like 2017's *Whitney: Can I Be Me?* and 2018's *Whitney* provide a clear picture of the forces that shaped Houston's ascent and decline.

Gerrick Kennedy's 2022 book *Didn't We Almost Have It All: A Defense of Whitney Houston* goes even further, examining Houston's rise and fall through the cultural lens of the 1980s and '90s and then reexamining them through the lens of today's Black Lives Matter (BLM) and LGBTQ+ movements. What emerges is a new clarity: Houston's demise cannot be reduced to her own self-destructive impulses, nor can it be chalked up to a single bad decision. We contributed too, through our racism, our pervasive misogyny and homophobia, and the way we condoned child abuse and stigmatized mental illness, shamed addiction, and both hungered for and fed tabloid culture.

At the beginning of her life, Houston was groomed for success by her mother, soul and gospel singer Cissy Houston, then packaged as a pop star by Arista Records mogul Clive Davis. When *TIME* magazine crowned Houston "the prom queen of soul," she lost the ability to define herself.[2]

MTV considered Houston too Black. The Rev. Al Sharpton and others accused her of not being Black enough, Sharpton even going so far as to call her "Whitey" Houston. In the late '80s, she was very audibly booed at the Soul Train Awards. In 1992 she was denied credit for breaking down racial barriers when she starred opposite Kevin Costner in the interracial romance *The Bodyguard*.[3] While some audiences applauded Houston for "transcending" race, others chastised her for abandoning it.

Adding to the pressure of having to sustain a career by

appealing to everyone was the weight of having to carry her extended family, including her brothers, Gary and Michael. Like Whitney, they too had survived unacknowledged childhood abuse by a family member and developed advanced substance abuse disorders years before they became part of her touring entourage.

Like O'Connor and Tina Turner, Houston rose above her circumstances on the exceptional strength of her voice. Yet her grievous arc was more or less drawn the day she signed her recording contract with Davis at age nineteen. She returned to the apartment that she shared with girlfriend Robyn Crawford and told her they would have to end their relationship. It was the only way, Houston reasoned, for either one of them to succeed.[4]

Although Houston continued to be questioned relentlessly about their relationship and was dogged by rumors that she was a lesbian, Crawford remained by her side, first as her personal assistant, then as her creative director and friend. That might have been enough had it not been for Houston's tumultuous marriage to "bad boy" Bobby Brown. But after Brown forced Crawford out of Houston's life in the late 1990s, her drug use intensified and her "good girl" image was no longer able to paper over intensifying struggles that culminated in her death in 2012, at the age of 48, from a drug overdose.

I'm not saying that the closet killed Houston, or that Bobby Brown did. What I am saying is that if Houston had been able to love whom she wanted to, to be the person that she wanted to be, and to make the music she wanted to make, her story might not have ended the same tragic way. The point is, we'll never know, because Whitney Houston was never allowed to be Whitney Houston. She became a pop sensation at the cost of becoming her own person. The same goes for many other female pop artists: Janet Jackson, Britney Spears, and Amy Winehouse, to name just a few. We built them up and knocked them down, without ever acknowledging the destructive force of our demands.

Even Madonna, who seemed to have mastered the game, in 2016 at *Billboard*'s Women in Music event for the first time publicly acknowledged how the industry's treatment of women affected her career and her psyche.[5] "I was of course inspired by Debbie Harry and Chrissie Hynde and Aretha Franklin, but my real muse was David Bowie," she said. "He embodied male and female spirit and that suited me just fine. He made me think there were no rules. But I was wrong. There are no rules — if you're a boy. There are rules if you're a girl."[6]

Then Madonna shockingly came out and named those rules: "If you're a girl, you have to play the game. You're allowed to be pretty and cute and sexy. But don't act too smart. Don't have an opinion that's out of line with the status quo. You are allowed to be objectified by men and dress like a slut, but don't own your sluttiness. And do not, I repeat do not, share your own sexual fantasies with the world. Be what men want you to be, but more importantly, be what women feel comfortable with you being around other men. And finally, do not age. Because to age is a sin. You will be criticized and vilified and definitely not played on the radio."

Madonna went on to say that the most controversial thing she had ever done was to stick around. She wasn't just talking about her career, but about her actual survival. Then, she urged women to form alliances of support for and with each other rather than aligning themselves with powerful men and their interests—suggesting that she had made missteps and had regrets about them.

I doubt that Miley Cyrus took that advice in, but others are doing so—look at millennial and Gen Z bands such as boygenius, Our Native Daughters, and the Highwomen as examples. These aren't novelty acts, or naïve displays of rosy-eyed feminist unity, but rather radical rethinkings of what a band could be outside of the male-dominated misogynistic system.

Although it is no longer the powerful monolith it once was, the industry still holds sway.[7] Metrics like streams and social media engagements have largely replaced the men in suits in major label decision-making, but if anything, the industry has become more creatively risk-averse, which makes change even more difficult to accomplish. The solution isn't simply to improve messaging, giving lip service to diversity and inclusion and promising to amplify the voices of women. Nor is it to encourage women to join bands or to create pipelines in production or management positions within the industry. Bringing anyone into a structurally dysfunctional system is likely to reward those who are willing to uphold that system and disempower those who seek to dismantle it.

Real change is going to require something like a "defund the industry" approach—and rebuilding it from the ground up; backing up commitments to achieving equality of opportunity with representation, resources, and support; and recognizing that doing so is good for business rather than antithetical to it. Or artists may choose to abandon the industry as we know it altogether, trying out new models such as short-term profit-sharing collectives. Whatever the future looks like, if we're not serious about cutting out the bullshit, as insiders and music fans, we'll get the system we pay for.

As those who have been harmed by that system have connected with each other and shared their stories, they've become better equipped to push back against underrepresentation and misrepresentation, exposing the music industry's abusive tactics and doing more to hold abusers accountable.[8] We now have a much deeper understanding of how entrenched power dynamics have historically contributed to the making and unmaking of female artists, and how stigma and the fear of stigma have been used to keep women from speaking out and advocating for themselves, which amounts to abuse upon abuse.

We're no longer as shocked when someone names their abuser.[9] But it's telling that some accused abusers, such as Marilyn Manson and Dr. Luke, are successfully pushing back in court and in the court of public opinion. Others, like Ryan Adams, are creeping back onto the stage. Many abusers have still not been named, the ones whose names have been floating around for years. They continue to work with impunity, often publicly aligning themselves with female artists and/or feminist causes, broadcasting that they're the nicest guys, and getting women to vouch for them as allies. Even though I hate to say it, there are some women in the industry who are just as toxic, women in positions of leadership—and, sadly, in mentorship.

I know that I've been talking explicitly about women in this chapter, but it's important to be clear that misogyny isn't only something experienced by people who were assigned female at birth, nor is it expressed exclusively by those who were not. Like racism, homophobia, and classism, misogyny is a system of mediation that carves us up and distorts us, keeps the disempowered on the margins, unseen and unheard. For that to change, we need to talk about all of it, even and especially the parts that are hardest to acknowledge.

WE NEED TO TALK ABOUT PRINCE

Which is why we need to talk about Prince. I want to say from the outset that I believe Prince was a musical genius who transcended boundaries and inspired others to soar, often lifting them up with his own wings. But I also think it's important to point out that Prince succeeded in doing those things because he was the master of his own image.

Born in 1958, the same year as Michael Jackson, Prince broke through rock's racist barrier at roughly the same time. His first attempt, like Jackson's, was not successful.[1] Although he was personally invited by Mick Jagger to open for the Rolling Stones at the LA Coliseum in 1981, when Prince took the stage in a see-through jacket, thigh-high boots, and black bikini pants, the headlining act's 90,000-plus audience was not receptive.

Even though Prince's setlist leaned toward the rock spectrum of his repertoire, with songs like "Bambi" and "When You Were Mine," the audience booed, shouting racist and homophobic rants, then started pelting Prince and his band with food and bottles. Promoter Bill Graham jumped onstage, trying to calm the audience, but to no avail. By the fourth song, Prince was forced to leave the stage, understandably distraught by the experience.

Jagger urged him to return two days later, but that time it went only slightly better. Prince closed the set with

"Why You Wanna Treat Me So Bad?" then later described the crowd as "tasteless in music and mentally retarded."

However, like Michael Jackson, he refused to be boxed in by his race. Prince's 1982 song "Little Red Corvette" got airplay on rock radio, which helped him to get his videos on MTV. White music critics started giving their blessings, hailing him as the next Jimi Hendrix. Prince and his multi-racial, multigender band started seeing bigger crowds at their shows, and more white faces in those crowds.

Prince started looking for the right vehicle to take his career to the next level without sacrificing control over his image or sound. Finding inspiration in Elvis's *Love Me Tender* and *Blue Hawaii* and the Beatles's *A Hard Day's Night* and *Help*, Prince saw the path forward as a feature movie, telling his managers that if they couldn't get him a deal, they'd be fired.[2]

They succeeded, but the budget for *Purple Rain* was minuscule, the director and producer were first-timers, and so were the stars, who were recruited from Prince's inner circle. Instead of Hollywood, the movie would be shot in Minneapolis — in the dead of winter.

In the film, Prince plays a version of himself, a struggling Minneapolis-based musician called "The Kid." Like the real-life Prince, he escapes a tumultuous homelife through music. He avoids repeating the sins of his father, the failed musician Francis L., a stand-in for Prince's real-life father, John Lewis Nelson. Overcoming his fear of obscurity, the Kid gets the fans and the girl. Life imitates art, or so it seemed at that time.

But when I watched *Purple Rain* again recently, I noticed a lot that had escaped me as a fourteen-year-old, namely, that this movie is at base about intergenerational trauma.

The Kid's father is haunted by his obscurity, the implicit reason why he constantly drinks and beats up his wife. The Kid's main rival, Morris Day, is a serial womanizer who orders his sidekick to toss a woman into a dumpster, and he does so without so much as a blink. For his part, the Kid doesn't treat women any better than these guys.

When his love interest, Apollonia, asks him to help her launch her own musical career, he invites her on a motor-cycle ride, then takes her out to a lake, where he tells her that she will first need to purify herself. After Apollonia disrobes and dives into the freezing water, he tells her she's in the wrong lake and speeds away. When he comes back for her, he warns Apollonia "not to get his seat all wet." Back at his place, which is also his parents' basement, the Kid's idea of foreplay is playing a cassette tape of a woman crying and teasing that he's the cause. Somehow this works for Apollonia, whose backstory remains untold.

Although the First Avenue club where the Kid performs is a New Wave utopia where audiences of all races and genders share a penchant for asymmetrical hairstyles and makeup, the Kid has major creative tensions with Wendy, his female guitarist, who's collaborated with Lisa, his nearly silent female keyboardist, on a song called "Slow Groove." The Kid refuses to listen to it, calling their music "stupid" and making immature jokes with the guys in the band about how Wendy must be on her period.

Wendy's backstage ballsiness vanishes when she's onstage miming fellatio on the Kid's guitar. Meanwhile Apollonia takes his rival, Morris Day, up on his offer to help her assemble a lingerie-clad girl group. Apollonia hocks her jewelry to buy the Kid a new phallic-looking guitar, but when she tells him she's working with Morris

Day, he strikes her. She's soon riding in Morris Day's limo wearing a slave collar.

Jump-cut to the Kid's father, whose botched suicide attempt serves as a warning to the Kid that he must change his ways or he'll wind up just like the old man. But it's only when the Kid is threatened with the ultimate humiliation — being replaced by the girl group — that he finally listens to his female bandmates. He uses their ideas as the basis for a slow-burner called "Purple Rain," which he dedicates to dear old dad and plays on the phallic-looking guitar to win back the crowd and Apollonia. The movie ends with the Kid's guitar ejaculating a purple ray into the audience.

When *Purple Rain* came out in 1984, not every critic thought it was brilliant. Pauline Kael decried its "flashy, fractured rock-video moments."[3] Vincent Canby called it "probably the first album cover ever to be released as a movie."[4] But insofar as *Purple Rain* put Prince in the megaplex, it was mission accomplished. In contrast with Michael Jackson, who seemed to lack sexuality altogether, Prince was dripping with a raw, androgynous, gender-fluid, racially ambiguous sexuality that twelve- to thirty-four-year-old white audiences registered as titillating and cultural conservatives registered as dangerous.

One of the songs from the film and the accompanying soundtrack album, "Darling Nikki," thumped and grinded with such sonic intensity, and its lyrics were so saturated with raunch, that it led a pearl-clutching Tipper Gore to form the Parents Music Resource Center (PMRC). The express goal of the organization was to protect impressionable children by censoring what it deemed the Filthy Fifteen. "Darling Nikki" topped the list. When the PMRC failed to censor Prince's music outright, it pushed the industry to slap a warning label on it, which only made it, and by extension, Prince, more desirable.

Like Madonna, Prince didn't run away from the taboo — he leaned into it, creating an outré hypersexual persona that defied norms, while at the same time living out a rags-to-riches tale as old and relatable as the American Dream. But while Madonna courted the press, Prince didn't grant interviews. He kept people guessing at his identity while keeping a very tight lid on his mysterious private life. He may have sung, "I'm not a woman / I'm not a man / I am something that you'll never understand," but the plain truth is he was able to achieve an edge in the industry — as in *Purple Rain* — because he was a man.

When Prince decided to break from his label in the early 1990s, the move wasn't only about maintaining creative control, the freedom to release as much material as he wanted, or retaining ownership of his master recordings. Adopting "the Love Symbol," which included elements of Mars and Venus, male and female, wasn't merely donning a stage moniker or a statement of identity. Nor were his various alter egos and aliases, such as Christopher and Camille. These were all expressions of Prince's refusal to allow others to define his identity, not so much to obscure it, but to expand it.

Prince succeeded in becoming the author of his own story, building himself into an indecipherable and thus unimpeachable glyph. Consider that everyone seemed, or pretended to seem, shocked when he died from an opioid overdose, citing his strictly clean lifestyle. Consider how quick many people were to attribute his drug use to pain management rather than even consider the possibility that it was addiction.

Our perceptions of Prince, like those of O'Connor, are

heavily filtered by power structures that shape public narratives. But even with all of the mediation, it's clear from what has trickled out over the years that the power dynamics between Prince and his protégés were complicated by several factors.

One was that those protégés were often his lovers.[5] A second was that in many cases they were significantly younger, sometimes even in their teens. But perhaps most significant of all was that these relationships were never egalitarian. Prince quietly managed to extend his need for control to others in his orbit, including the women whose careers he elevated.[6]

Prince's former chauffeur once described a bizarre three-hour date with Sheena Easton in which Prince insisted that she communicate with him only through her eyes.[7] Charlene Friend says Prince made Friend call him "Messiah" and believed that if you had sex with him, you became one with him.[8]

She and Jill Jones both publicly accused Prince of being emotionally, physically, and sexually abusive, the latter telling a journalist, "Has he been abusive to me? Yes. But Prince used to give me these incredible gifts. Just after doing something horrible. When he offered me a car after *Purple Rain*, I always wondered what was going to happen, what will fall on my head, which shoe will fly in the air. What will he ask me or do to me in exchange? When you loved Prince, it had a cost. Everything had a cost. And you had to be ready to give everything, even your fucking dignity."[9]

That trade-off appeared to be the case even with his band the Revolution. When Lisa Coleman came to audition, she observed that Prince had a poster of "A Star Is Born" hanging on his wall.[10] Although he introduced

"Purple Rain" as "a song that the girls in the band wrote" in the film, he did not credit the real-life Wendy and Lisa as songwriters, nor did he acknowledge their hand in transforming "Purple Rain" from its origins as a country ballad intended as a collaboration with Stevie Nicks into the song that helped make him a megastar.[11]

After Prince abruptly broke up the Revolution in 1986, he also failed to credit them for their contributions to his 1987 release *Sign o' the Times*.[12] When he took a religious turn at the end of the 1990s, Prince offered Wendy and Lisa a spot on a Revolution reunion tour, but it fell apart when they learned it was contingent on attending a press conference where Wendy Melvoin would denounce her lesbian sexuality and announce that she'd become a Jehovah's Witness.[13]

Although Prince undeniably expanded expressions of gender and sexuality in the '80s and '90s, he had expressed a different attitude as far back as 1979, when on "Bambi" he sang about trying to convince a woman to abandon her female lover because "it's better with a man." He ends the song with: "Bambi, I know what you need/Bambi, maybe you need to bleed."

After his religious awakening, Prince became unambiguously antigay. In a 2008 interview with the *New Yorker*, he "tapped his Bible" and said, "God came to Earth and saw people sticking it wherever and doing it with whatever, and he just cleared it all out. He was, like, 'Enough.'"[14] In his 2013 song "Da Bourgeoisie," Prince sings: "Yesterday I saw you kickin' it with another girl / You was all wrapped up around her waist / Last time I checked, you said you left the dirty world . . . I guess a man's only good for a rainy day / Maybe you're just another bearded lady at the cabaret."

In 2014, as a guest on the short-lived reboot of Arsenio Hall's show, Prince was asked by an audience member to name a pet peeve. With a smile he complained about strangers trying to touch his hair, and then visibly cringed in disgust when he added that most of those strangers were "dudes."[15]

I know I'm telling you things you probably don't want to hear, especially about someone who isn't able to respond. We don't want salacious rumors to bring down someone who has done so much to bring others up. We don't want to believe that someone we admire deeply might not be the flawless deity we want or need them to be. But the truth is that none of us knows what really went on behind the closed doors at Paisley Park, after the stage lights went dark and Prince was no longer performing Prince. And that's my point.

In 2014, O'Connor renewed her accusations against Prince in a Norwegian radio interview, and then again in 2021 with the publication of her memoir.[16] These accusations were made in the context of a long, terrible, and tragic history of white women falsely accusing Black men and even boys of predation and assault, from the Scottsboro Boys to Emmett Till to the Exonerated Five. In 2020, Christian Cooper couldn't even go bird-watching in Central Park without a white woman calling 911 to falsely report that he was threatening her and her dog.

The reaction among Prince's fanbase was swift and unforgiving: No way he did this. If he did this, why is she just bringing this up now, all these years later? She's just a stupid, crazy one-hit-wonder bitch who got rich off his song, and now she's saying this shit about him? Ungrateful bald-headed psycho. If not for him, no one would even know who she was.[17]

Here's the thing: O'Connor was never Prince's protégé. He did not and could not control her repertoire, her finances, the way she spoke to the press or the public, or the way she spoke to him privately. It's not a stretch for me to imagine how that made him feel because I've seen that movie, Prince's movie, a movie that reflected its protagonist and the culture.[18]

Everyone saw the genius but seemed to miss that the Kid hurt other people because he was hurting. Very few people criticized Prince for the violence perpetrated against women in *Purple Rain* because that's just how things were in 1984. But they're not that way anymore. And we can't keep giving Prince and other alleged abusers an automatic pass.

Isn't it possible for us to love Prince as an artist and applaud him for opening doors, while at the same time asking ourselves why we are so reluctant to question his personal conduct, to dismiss even the possibility that women who have claimed that he mistreated them might be telling the truth?

Why do we extend the benefit of the doubt to Prince but not O'Connor? Why are we so primed to buy into the idea that he's a flawless genius and she's a flawed psycho?

If we can love Prince's music without loving or accepting everything he's ever done, it's also possible for us to love O'Connor's music without loving or accepting everything she's ever done. It's only when we accept her full humanity that we can arrive at an authentic understanding and compassion for our own humanity. If we love the tear that O'Connor sheds in the video for "Nothing Compares 2 U," we also have to be willing to acknowledge and address the pain that provoked it.

HURT PEOPLE HURT

I really want to tell you that O'Connor somehow overcame everything—the abuse, the double standard, the drama, and demons of her own making. But this is not a revision, or a do-over. It is a sincere attempt to understand another person's suffering, indeed our own suffering as a society.

I believe it's that suffering that fueled her misogynist Facebook rant in July 2015 against Kim Kardashian, wherein she asks, "What is this cunt doing on the cover of Rolling Stone? Music has officially died. Who knew it would be Rolling Stone that murdered it? Simon Cowell and Louis Walsh can no longer be expected to take all the blame. Bob Dylan must be fucking horrified. #BoycottRollingStone."

I believe suffering is also what led her to post about an emotional breakdown she had a month later and attributed to being denied hormone replacement therapy after an emergency hysterectomy. "I was flung into surgical menopause," she wrote. "Hormones were everywhere. I became very suicidal. I was a basket case."

And I think it's probably what's behind what happened a year later, when O'Connor was staying with friends in suburban Chicago, volunteering as a companion at a veterans hospital and undergoing intensive mental health counseling while in the midst of a custody battle with Dónal Lunny over their son, Shane.

The Irish Children's and Family Welfare Agency, Tusla, had ordered that her visits with Shane be supervised, and then rescinded them altogether, taking him into their care. In response, O'Connor publicly threatened suicide and lashed out against John Reynolds, and their son, Jake, accusing them of abandoning her.

In May 2016, a month after Prince died, O'Connor posted on Facebook that Arsenio Hall had supplied him with drugs— information that she said she had also given to the authorities investigating Prince's death. She referenced her own history with Hall, publicly warning him, "They are aware you spiked me years ago at Eddie murphy's [sic] house. You best get tidying your man cave."

A week later, O'Connor was reported missing after she went out for a bike ride, later that day posting a series of troubling Facebook messages from an unknown location, prompting concern for her safety. Although she was found safe at a local hotel later that day, her troubles were far from over.[1] Hall denied the allegations O'Connor had made and slapped her with a $5 million defamation suit.[2] (The matter was settled privately in February 2017 after O'Connor agreed to retract the statements and issue an apology.) She was also being sued by Fachtna O'Ceallaigh for defamation and breach of contract dating back to the events of 2012.[3]

O'Connor checked herself into a rehab facility in San Francisco, which she said was to treat her thirty-plus-year addiction to marijuana, then she flew back briefly to Ireland, then to New Jersey, where she could be close to her manager and receive psychiatric treatment.

At some point on this timeline, O'Connor was reportedly forced to sell her home in Ireland to settle her debts, including unpaid taxes in the hundreds of thousands of dollars.[4] She also had to sell the masters from her first four albums to Universal Music Group.[5] She changed her name to Magda Davitt, a decision she explained as an expression of her desire to "be free of patriarchal slave names."

Then, in August 2017, O'Connor posted the now famous twelve-minute Facebook video from the New Jersey motel where she'd holed up for weeks. "I hope this video is somehow helpful," a teary O'Connor began, "not only to me, but I know that I'm only one of millions and millions and millions of people in the world that are just like me actually."

O'Connor spoke of her loneliness, the stigma, the way her pain had been used to hurt her and invalidate her. She said she wanted to be with her mother, for her kids to come get her, for someone to take care of her, for people to see what it is like to suffer from mental illness. She demanded compassion, knowing that it would likely never come.

Dr. Phil got wind of O'Connor's situation and reached out with an offer to arrange treatment at a trauma treatment facility in the South where he was affiliated. She told the *Independent* his call made her feel like "Cinderella" and only later realized that he exploited her.[6] Apparently she didn't know or had forgotten about Dr. Phil's offer to "help" Britney Spears.

O'Connor says she agreed to be interviewed for an hour on his talk show before receiving any treatment, but then he disappeared without any further involvement.[7] When things didn't work out with the first treatment center, she was flown to another one in Los Angeles. Then John Reynolds flew to the United States and brought her back to Ireland, where she reentered intensive therapy.

This might have been the end of the story and, all things considered, not necessarily a bad one. But sometimes the story you want and the story you get aren't the same thing. And sometimes you just have to figure out what kind of story you can live with.

When I first started working in music journalism, I wouldn't have said that out loud. If you heard my stories, you heard only the sound of my voice, and perhaps my name in the byline, and you may have made assumptions about me. In the days when NPR had public commenting, guys would often post praise for my work—wow, a chick who knows about rock!

If you've spent any time at the movies, it makes sense that you might be under the misimpression that chicks who know about rock are merely groupies with notebooks. From *A Star is Born* and *Annie Hall* to *The Doors*, *Hot Tub Time Machine*, and *Rock of Ages*, they're only in the picture to suck the male rock star's cock, literally and/or figuratively. If not, they're ambitious fame-chasers who use their feminine wiles to get the scoop and get ahead. A "chick who knows about rock" who doesn't do either of those things is cool . . . or scary, depending on whose needs she's serving.

As I navigated that minefield, I consciously remained behind the curtain, avoiding self-promotion, parking handles on Twitter and later Instagram just so that no one else grabbed them, joining Facebook only nominally. But over time, editors, managers, publicists, and other gatekeepers started recognizing my name. Artists let me see them as they really are.

I started to see myself differently, too, as I really am, as someone who has the ability—and the responsibility—to report on what had been overlooked, forgotten, distorted, or never told at all. Being a truth-teller meant revealing parts of my own story too, how I got to be the person on the mic.

Perhaps unsurprisingly, showing more of myself in my work was met with some resistance from total strangers, people who went through the trouble to find me online and email me through the contact form on my website to tell me that I'm an idiot, a hack, a bitch, etc. Their messages could be insanely long, written in ALL CAPS, laced with hate-flirts, or just plain creepy.

In terms of content and scale, this was nothing compared to what O'Connor has had to endure over the years, although I will say it is hard to laugh it off or shut it out entirely—especially when people are griping about things that are completely beyond my control—the headline chosen without my knowledge or consent, the minor typo in an autogenerated transcript, the nonessential detail that got cut at the last minute for lack of time. The purpose of their feedback isn't constructive. It's to shut me up or shut me down. I get it.

That's why what I'm about to tell you feels so scary. I worry that it will be weaponized. People won't see me anymore as a competent journalist, but as someone who's been damaged and is therefore unstable and untrustworthy. It feels unsafe emotionally because when people feel bad for me, it feels like pity, and pity feels like shame. When your family is messed up, you worry the world will see you as messed up, and they'll invalidate you. But the only way that's going to change is to talk about it.

When I was six, my aunt died. She killed herself, actually, right before the holidays. I didn't know her very well, only that she was very sick. My mother told me that my aunt would answer the door naked when my grandfather came over and carelessly scarf down handfuls of pills while worrying incessantly that eating old lettuce would kill her. My mother would wind her finger around her ear, a short-hand way of explaining that my aunt was crazy.

I wouldn't learn until I was in my teens that my aunt was bipolar, that she spent years in and out of psychiatric institutions, and that she died from a medication overdose. My mother told me only that my aunt had died in her sleep and then barely spoke of her sister ever again.

I was terrified and couldn't sleep. I had lots of questions about what had happened, but my mother gave me no answers. Then she finally presented me with a tattered little book, which was odd, since she never gave me anything.

There were some creepy-looking kids on the cover, blond and rosy-cheeked, holding open a prayer book. The title read *Prayers for Children*. Why was she giving me this? I wasn't raised in any religion. I never once saw her or my father pray. No one I knew prayed or looked like those kids.

She explained to me that she got the book when she was about my age. It was a gift from one of the customers who came into her father's corner store in Devil's Pocket. That was weird too. All she had ever told me about the store was how awful it and the customers were. Still, there must have been a reason she kept that book, and a reason she thought it was time for me to have it. I scurried up the stairs to my room and started flipping through the pages.

I found one called "Bedtime Prayer." That must be it! On the left side was a picture of a kid with angel wings and on the other were two more winged kids putting a blanket over a cradle. I noticed the baby's eyes were closed and its rattle was tossed aside on the floor. Like all the other kids in the book, they were blond and rosy-cheeked. Then I started reading the words.

"Now I lay me down to sleep, I pray thee Lord my soul to keep, if I should die before I wake, I pray thee Lord my soul to take . . ."

Pray thee Lord my soul to take? Is that what happened to my aunt? My mother had told me that I was crazy many times, crazy for not liking Barbie dolls, crazy for "making" my father hit me, crazy for not being who she wanted or needed me to be: normal. Was my mother trying to tell me that the Lord would come and take my soul too? Was this what happened to "crazy" people?

I barely left my room after reading "Bedtime Prayer." I just kept all the lights on and rocked in my bed, frozen with fear. My mother either didn't notice or pretended she didn't notice. That was her way. My father could have killed me in any one of his blind rages, and she would have let him.

Eventually, S, who lived next door, came by asking if I could come out and play. I told her no. She asked why, so I brought her upstairs and showed her the book. She said, "Give me that thing."

Now this girl, S, was a tough kid, much tougher than me. She had to be. Her father was this little, quiet guy, but to my young eyes her mother appeared to be a raging hulk with hair just like Cruella de Vil. Whenever she wanted S to come home, she would pile herself into her huge black Cadillac and go careening down the alley, screaming S's name while all the other kids scampered out of the way.

S dragged me and the book into that alley. She pointed at the cover, at the cherubic kids, and angels, and the lamb. She shook her head and said, "That's bullshit." Then she chucked the book to the ground, and off we went to play. Problem solved, but only sort of.

In that moment I started to realize I'd lost not only my aunt but my mother too, or at least the illusion that I ever had a mother. I mean, what is a mother if not someone to look after you, to love and protect you—and, if she can't do that, at least to give you a sense that you are worthy of being loved and protected?

After that I stayed away from home as much as possible. I became that kid that other families set out another place for at dinner, that kid who hopes no one notices that the clothing she's wearing is always out of style or doesn't fit because it's a hand-me-down from someone she never knew, that kid whose parents don't show up for anything. Ever.

Lies, liars, and abuse. If my mother had been religious, I might well have saved that book as a symbol of her hypocrisy, and if I had the chance as an adult, I would have destroyed it on live TV, too, ripped it to shreds, showing the world that the perpetuation of intergenerational abuse could certainly not be what God intended.

That book never left the alley, but I did. When I was six, I started running, and in some ways, I never stopped. Figuring out how to survive without a mother was the easy part. Figuring out how to mourn is something I'm still working on.

TRUTHFUL WITNESS

Surviving a wound that deep informs my reading of O'Connor, though to be honest, I don't understand every single part of her story. I don't know why her need to be an ally is so strong that it can sometimes appear to be an appropriation of other people's struggles, why she makes false equivalences or traffics in stereotypes without even necessarily realizing it, and why she often seems to court controversy despite the suffering that inevitably follows.

But I do understand what it feels like to need to hear a voice that sounds like a blanket, a songbook that you can wrap around yourself to hide from your pain. I get the part about wanting to become that voice for other people, and the part about why no blanket can ever be strong enough to shield you or anyone else from the troubles of the world. But most of all, I get why you need to keep trying, not in spite of but because of it all.

After asking, in an open letter, for Pope Francis to excommunicate her, as she had previously asked two of his predecessors, O'Connor reverted to Islam in 2018. She took the new name Shuhada Davitt, later Shuhada Sadaqat. She posted a photo of herself on Twitter wearing a hijab, which shocked people more than they were shocked by her shaved head, her destruction of the photograph of the pope, or her sexual want ads combined. Predictably, they pounced all over her.

O'Connor then made several controversial comments criticizing Jewish and Christian theologians, and referring to non-Muslims as "disgusting."[1] She later clarified that the comments were only made in an intentional effort to be bounced from Twitter. Then in 2019 she formally apologized for the pain caused by her remarks, this time explaining that they were made as a reaction to the Islamophobia she experienced when she made her reversion public.

She started performing in Europe again, in her hijab, in the place where she'd always been most herself—on the stage, where it's just her and her songs and her audience. She even started singing "Nothing Compares 2 U" again—a song she'd sworn off performing for years because she said it triggered her memories of being assaulted by Prince. A few dates turned into more, then into plans for a US expansion, an album, and the completion of a memoir that had long been in the works.

O'Connor set out on a quiet tour of the American West Coast in early 2020, playing eight shows over twelve days—many sold out, the seats filled with fans, not industry VIPs. The set list was seventeen songs long, mostly made up of crowd-pleasing hits. She was in fine form.[2] Kathleen Hanna, who caught O'Connor's performance in Los Angeles, remarked, "To say it was religious would be an understatement."

In 2020 O'Connor was no longer waifish or fragile. She looked like a prize fighter, with a voice that was deeper, steelier, weathered, and, most of all, earned. She looked the way I imagine the girls I grew up with would look now if they have survived into their middle age.

When O'Connor sang barefoot in her hijab and burqa, her expression was buoyant and triumphant, showing that she still had the fire, that she was not just going through the motions or taking a victory lap. Her new name, Shuhada, means "truthful witness." She appeared to be saying to her admirers and her detractors, "This is me. This is who I am. I have been through it all and I am still standing, still singing, still demanding to be heard." It almost came across as a dare—I dare you to try and stop me from my truth.

Plans to expand the tour to coincide with the thirtieth anniversary of *I Do Not Want What I Haven't Got* were called off when the coronavirus pandemic put live performing on pause. But O'Connor maintained her momentum, releasing a cover of gospel singer and civil rights activist Mahalia Jackson's "Trouble of the World" as a benefit for BLM in October 2020.

In a press statement, she said she thought the song was not about death or dying, but rather "a message of certainty that the human race is on a journey toward making this world paradise and that we will get there." She enlisted an old ally, Don Letts, to direct the music video for the song, which included footage from BLM protests in Peckham where O'Connor held up a placard of Jackson.

O'Connor went on to tease a new album, *No Veteran Dies Alone*, which was slated for release in 2022. But then another announcement came out: all of O'Connor's 2021 shows were to be postponed because she was entering into a yearlong rehabilitation program for trauma and addiction. She promised that her memoir would be published as planned in June 2021, and she made good on that promise. She dedicated the book to the staff and patients at St. Patrick's Hospital in Dublin, to her father, John O'Connor, to the publisher David Rosenthal, to Bob Dylan, and to Jeff

Rosen—Dylan's manager, who did eventually help her, in a way, by encouraging her to write her memoir.

So O'Connor wrote her book and now I've written mine. In between I managed to string miles and miles of tin cans together until they reached all the way across the ocean. When we Zoomed, I had so much to ask her, so many things that I wanted to say and couldn't say. After we went through all the standard interview questions, which she answered coherently and candidly, O'Connor and I spoke at some length about Dylan and his influence. At one point she started reciting some of his song titles, which I started scribbling down on a Post-it note.

As she ticked them off, she looked off to the side and her speech slowed. She seemed to be losing herself for a moment, as though she were reliving something, rather than just listing titles or remembering songs. After the interview, while I was waiting for her to send me the recording she'd made of her side of our conversation, I put together a playlist.[3] The next day I popped on my headphones and pulled it up as I started vacuuming my house—a chore I'd long neglected as I prepped for the call.

I'm not a crier. The cry was beaten out of me by my family, and by the culture I grew up in, where crying was akin to raising a flag of defeat. There was also all that stupid toxic working-class bullshit I saw in the movies—Rizzo in *Grease* and Philadelphia movies like *Rocky*: "It ain't about how hard you hit but how hard you can get hit and keep moving forward; how much you can take and keep moving forward" and so on, blah, blah, blah.

But I will tell you without shame that O'Connor's playlist made me burst into tears—a lifetime's worth. At that moment I realized that the songs were chapters of a larger story that could have gone over my head, in one ear and out the other. But remember all that stuff I told you at the beginning of this book, about how tuning your ear requires you to be in touch with your own experiences and emotions? I wasn't just hearing the words or the notes in those songs, but feeling the feelings — like Fiona Apple boxing around the mic as she belts out "The Whole of the Moon."

And then I was able to picture in the most detailed way what O'Connor spoke about in her memoir, starting with the image of O'Connor's brother coming home with the Dylan records, and then her in the shed, knees held up to her chest, rocking back and forth as the records went round and round on the turntable, looking at the album covers, at that face she said was so beautiful it was as if God blew a breath from Lebanon and it became a man. She called Dylan her savior; her name for him was "Lebanon Man."

And then I could hear the Lebanon Man singing, "Baby, please stop crying," and I thought of how the backup singers must have sounded just like angels to her, and how the sun must have come pouring in through the window. Then I heard "Shine your light on me," in "Precious Angel," and "But the enemy I see wears a cloak of decency" in "Slow Train," and on and on. I felt the weight of it all, but also the lift, the miracle of it.

This is the stuff I'm never supposed to tell you because it reveals that I'm too close, too invested, maybe even projecting my story onto hers. But maybe the opposite is true — that everyone else hasn't let themselves get close enough, they aren't invested enough, and their empathy has been snuffed out by false neutrality.

We journalists are often told that we should be guided by curiosity, but we're not told enough that we should also be guided by care and compassion, and the belief that what we are reporting can and does make a difference. Otherwise, why bother?

When my NPR story aired, I emailed O'Connor the link, and she wrote back immediately asking what people thought about it. NPR doesn't allow online commenting anymore, so I had no public reaction to share with her, but more to the point, I cared only that I got it right and that it got through to the people who needed to hear it. I told her that was all that mattered to me. I wished it was all that mattered to her.

Then people started reaching out to her on Twitter. Someone said something like "I heard Kathleen Hanna talking about you on WNYC." She wrote back right away "I friggin' love Kathleen Hanna," but it was clear she hadn't pieced together that Kathleen Hanna was talking about her in my profile, or that it was heard across all of NPR's member stations coast to coast.

"Well, how did they like it?" she wrote to me again. And I wanted to write back, "It doesn't fucking matter if they liked it. It matters that they heard it." I was crushed that she still gave a shit about what everybody thought, the clicks and the likes being confused for truth. I wanted to do for her what S did for me in the alley all those years ago, to help her see the falseness of an illusion, to free herself from the need for approval that will never come, the approval that shatters each time you seek it.

Most of the press O'Connor received for her memoir was actually favorable, but on the same day that my story aired, O'Connor appeared on BBC's "Woman's Hour." Instead of using the time, as O'Connor would have preferred, to highlight all of the ways she had been right — about the Catholic Church's abuse scandal, about the music industry, about her right to tell her own story — the show's host, Emma Barnett, asked her to respond to a review of her memoir by the *Telegraph*'s music critic Neil McCormick, who had referred to her reputation as "the crazy lady in pop's attic." O'Connor fired back, "It's not like I'm trying to attack people with knives or trying to strangle people while I'm walking around in my nightdress."

Although O'Connor seemed okay with the rest of the interview, after the show she took to Twitter to condemn Barnett's interview as "extremely offensive and even misogynistic." She vowed never to appear on "Woman's Hour" again. Then she posted another tweet, this one an apology for comments she had made in response to Barnett's question about having four children by four different men. On the show O'Connor blurted out, "Nobody bats an eyelid when Jamaican fellas have kids with fucking — sorry didn't mean to say that — they have kids with tons of people and no one bats an eyelid."

In her attempt to clarify her comments, she tweeted, "Also, apologies if I accidentally offended Jamaican men. I was referring to specific friends of mine in the music business. Jamaican people are my favourite people on this earth and Jamaican male musicians my biggest inspiration."

The well-meaning but cringy apology reverberated across the internet. Over the next few weeks, O'Connor put out statements announcing that she was pulling out of further press interviews and promotional appearances for her memoir, then that she had decided to quit the music business altogether, then that she was retracting her previous statement, which she described as a response to being rankled by journalists.

Then she retracted that statement and said she was retiring after all, later that summer announcing that she was going to write an opinion column for an Irish newspaper. Better to be on the side of writing about people rather than them writing about her, I thought. It seemed like a good way to be a public figure without being a public figure.

But then, in January 2022, along with the rest of the world, I heard the news of her son Shane's death. I immediately thought back to what she'd said about being a mom in her memoir and in our interview. It was a matter of pride for O'Connor that she was able to raise her children and have close relationships with them, even though her relationship with her own mother had been so profoundly troubled. She was particularly close with Shane, who — as they say in Ireland — was the spit of her.

Losing a child would be a tragedy for any parent. Even worse, Shane had taken his own life. And even worse than that is to experience such a devastating loss as a mother who had to overcome the impact of her own upbringing to bring her children up right, as loved and valued, and worthy of living. In a series of heart-wrenching tweets, O'Connor blamed herself.

Like her, I'm a mother who didn't really have a mother, who knows what it's like to feel the weight of having children of your own, of knowing that no matter what else you do in your life, the one thing you must not fuck up, cannot fuck up, is being a mother. Is it any wonder that so many women who are abused as kids either don't have any kids or have lots of kids? Think about it.

O'Connor said that after her mother died, she couldn't

go back to Ireland for thirteen years, and cried for twenty-five. After I left Philadelphia for Hampshire College, I declared myself a functional orphan, took a new name, and tried for decades to emancipate myself from the scars wrought by my father's fists and the voice of my mother telling me that I was nothing and deserved nothing, and that nothing good would ever come from anything I tried. But that meant that every accomplishment, every accolade, everything in my life that ever worked out right felt at best like a dodged bullet. It could all just vanish or turn to dust and somehow it would all be my fault.

It took a lot of work to realize that instead of running away, I needed to start circling back and reclaiming parts of myself, even the broken parts that I have to learn to love as though I am my own mother.

A big part of what changed in me was becoming a mother myself, and feeling like I needed to give my children a sense of context — not about where they came from but where I came from — who that kid was, and *why* she was. So I went back to Philadelphia, first by myself, and then with my wife and kids.

They don't need to witness or process all of my feelings about it. Just being there with me is enough for me to know that I haven't totally fucked it all up, that there is a way out of the shadow and into the light, into something that feels like hope.

When I heard about Shane's death, I emailed O'Connor a brief condolence letter, then got an auto-reply saying that she was temporarily deactivating her email account. Good, I thought, I hope she's getting the support she's going to need. Then came a series of troubling tweets, then the media and the internet trolls coming out of the woodwork criticizing her for the outfit she wore to Shane's funeral, the cigarettes she left in his casket. Everything was a circus. AGAIN.

She blamed herself, of course; after all, it was she who tweeted out the funeral details, she who later said she did it because she didn't want to be alone. But hasn't that been the problem all along?

My heart truly breaks for her. Yes, O'Connor is a loose cannon, but she most often fires at herself. Remember what she said: "Nothing can touch me. I reject the world. Nobody can do a thing to me that hasn't been done already." That's no way to live, no way to heal.

Of course, I don't agree with everything she says, and sometimes I wish she would say less, but she has the right to be imperfect, mad even, to fight off the voices of others, to use her own voice as she sees fit.[4]

Just imagine if we all did that, a choir of millions of Sinéads busting out from all the rooms where we've been locked away and silenced, hearing each other the way she heard Dylan, knowing that believing in God isn't the same as believing in men, and that no matter how much we stumble, we all matter.

A few days after this all transpired, O'Connor deleted her Twitter account, then briefly reinstated it to apologize for upsetting people. She said she was going to the hospital but vowed that this was just a delay. She was going to find Shane, she said, and I believe her.

EPILOGUE

Writing a book is a largely solitary act, but as soon as I appeared on the podcast *You're Wrong About*, shortly before the May 2023 publication of *Why Sinéad O'Connor Matters*, I started receiving emails from around the world. Some listeners wrote about how Sinéad inspired them to speak out against injustice. Others recollected past trauma, what it meant for them to feel seen in her music and heard in the way I spoke about her.

The frequency and emotional charge of this outpouring intensified once the book came out. Whenever I visited bookstores, people stuck around wanting or needing to talk about Sinéad. Approaching me at times with tears in their eyes, they thanked me for writing the book, being a vocal and visible feminist queer reporter, and standing up for survivors. Once, a woman whose arm was inked with a massive tattoo of Sinéad in panoply, gave me a jacket pin that said, "Don't take any shit."

As this choir of Sinéads materialized, it felt uplifting, but also overwhelming. I realized I was becoming an unintentional and inadequate proxy for the living, breathing, Sinéad, and I often wondered what she would have made of this. Having decided early on that I was writing my book about her, and not *for her*, I never told Sinéad what I was doing, never sought her permission, and never asked for her endorsement. I have no idea if she knew how much love there was for her in my book or out there in the world.

I hoped someday to make it to Ireland with a suitcase full of correspondence that had been addressed to me, but was meant for her. Yes, Sinéad, they heard you and they liked it. I wished I could tell her how honored I felt to sit beside Vernon Reid at Rough Trade in Rockefeller Center as he recalled being in the audience the night she performed "War" and destroyed the photograph of Pope John Paul II on *SNL*, and how shaken I was when the *Washington Post*'s Geoff Edgers shared an unreleased demo of "Horse on the Highway," the mother's lament that she'd sent him when they toured together in 2020.

I wished I could describe to her the disorienting collision of past, present, and future I experienced on my tour stop in Philadelphia, where I read the excerpt from the book about running wild on South Street in a bookstore just around the corner from South Street. Maybe telling her about that part would be selfish, but then again, only Sinéad could truly understand it.

"What are you going to do next?" people often asked me, especially as the tour began to wind down in late June. Writing the book had shifted my priorities as a journalist, and journalism had been shifting too, diminished by wave after wave of layoffs, budget cuts, and programming cancellations. When NPR laid off roughly 10 percent of its staff in spring 2023 my editor encouraged me to keep bringing her new pitches, but cautioned that the culture desk was being restructured, which likely meant much less airtime—as little as two or three minutes per story. Then, on July 26, she sent me a text that changed everything: "Just saw that Sinéad O'Connor has died."

How was that possible? In February, Sinéad's version of "The Skye Boat Song" was released as the theme music for the seventh season of *Outlander*. In March, she made a widely publicized appearance, winning the inaugural RTÉ Choice Music Prize for Classic Irish Album with *I Do Not Want What I Haven't Got*. And in early July, she announced that she had moved to London to complete a new album, *No Veteran Dies Alone*. Teasing future tour plans on social media, she used the playful hashtag #TheBitchIsBack, and it appeared she was back, as ever the phoenix rising from the flame.

When Sinéad popped back up again to show fans around her new Herne Hill flat, she spoke about mourning Shane, and, yes, she appeared fragile. But she still looked very much alive, and I read her resurfacing as proof of her resilience. I also know there was a part of me that needed to see her as invincible, which is why it hit me so hard that she wasn't.

Stunned by my editor's text, I offered to put together a proper obituary immediately, but she told me NPR already had it covered in-house. At that very moment, my phone started blowing up with dozens of live TV and radio interview requests from other news outlets in the US, Ireland, England, and Canada. I also penned several written reflections overnight for publication in the morning, stepping into a role that I'd long resisted — that of truthful witness.

Ragged, raw, and reeling, I kept going nonstop over the next few weeks knowing there would be a limited window when all the world's attention would be focused on why Sinéad O'Connor matters — not the book, but its central argument that she was neither demon nor saint, but an incredibly courageous human whose music, life, and legacy were about so much more than a single song or act of defiance.

Of course, I wasn't alone in making that case or addressing the broader cultural implications, a reframing initiated by Sinéad's own 2021 memoir and extended by the Irish filmmaker Kathryn Ferguson's 2022 documentary *Nothing Compares*. As far as I'm concerned, the more everyone is talking about what Sinéad cared about and stood for, the better. I just want it to be real.

Although I appreciated that many celebrities flocked to social media to sing her posthumous praises, I wished that more of them had reached out to Sinéad when she was still alive. I was also heartened by many remembrances in the press, but heartbroken by a dense tangle of factually inaccurate misreporting on her life and salacious speculation about her death in some accounts. I got through the subsequent months not only with help from friends and family but also, in no small part, by talking about Sinéad with people I didn't know and reading the supportive emails they sent, and continue to send, nearly every day.

These interactions, even a simple "How are you?," showed me that our most painful, unexpected derailments can also bring about, as Sinéad called them, *rerailments* — realignments that put us in deeper connection with ourselves and others. As I began to envision the path forward, I noted that Sinéad's moves were never calculated, calibrated, performed for profit or for popularity. She lived her life as a bold dare that challenged me to own my unedited story and live it out loud. By inspiring me to fully embrace my authentic self, she helped me to experience happiness again as well as sorrow, and to thrive in the light of my own humanity at moments when the world felt its darkest. Now it's time to pay that forward.

Just as Sinéad believed the artist has a responsibility to be themselves at all costs, I believe the journalist has a responsibility to tell the truth at all costs. So, let me close with this: The truest expression of why Sinéad O'Connor matters is revealed not in what she alone achieved, but in what we can achieve together when we show up for each other. Some of us call this holding space, but lately I've been thinking about ways we can create shared space too, building a better future in the physical world as well as online and on air. I think of this as the space of possibility, where your hope gives me hope and your joy gives me joy.

No matter how alone she must have felt at various times in her life, Sinéad never stopped caring, never stopped trying to spark a dialogue about what's most difficult, calling us into the conversations we most need to have and the change that we most need to manifest. That's why it's not enough to applaud her as a brave warrior. We have to be brave and carry on the work of healing ourselves. Talking and listening to each other doesn't necessarily mean that the world will become a better place, but what if it could?

Allyson McCabe

ACKNOWLEDGMENTS

Parts of this story were informally auditioned for friends and family, people I know, and perfect strangers. More often than not, it began with a question: What do *you* think about Sinéad O'Connor? I'm grateful to the University of Texas Press for the chance to share what I think—and feel. In particular, my heartfelt thanks go to Casey Kittrell, Evelyn McDonnell, and two anonymous readers of the manuscript for engaging with my ideas and arguments, and for supporting me when I stepped out of my reporter comfort zone.

I didn't have a Sister Margaret in my young life, but I want to express my deep gratitude to all of the people I've named or referenced in this story, as well as the teachers in the Philadelphia MG program—Joy Kurtz, Joann Neufeld, and Ron Romoff—who taught me the difference between school and education. They showed me how to conjure wings with words and modeled for me how to be exceptional, which got me all the way to Yale and gave me the confidence to fly away from it, too.

Professionally, I'm indebted to Naomi Starobin, Tom Cole, and Ciera Crawford for putting me on the air and letting me sing in my own voice. The same goes for those who have supported this book, and its author, in countless ways: Rachel Angel, Bob Bumbera, Joe Castro, Myke

Dodge Weiskopf, Sadie Dupuis, Geoff Edgers, Amanda Hess, Jack Hitt, Jessica Hopper, Dan Kennedy, Sarah Klein, Kristen Kurtis, Gianna LaMorte, Joan LeMay, Angelica Lopez-Torres, Fiona Macdonald, Kimberly Mack, Sarah Marshall, Craig Marks, Shirley Manson, Brian McTear, Liane Nelson, Emmy Parker, Joel Pinckney, Margo Price, Vernon Reid, Inga Reznik, Daniel Sea, Tabassum Siddiqui, Zoe Strauss, Alex Suskind, Gayle Wald, Bruce Warren, Diana Weymar, Allison Wolfe, Kathy Valentine, and Sharon Van Etten.

On a personal note, I want to thank my kids, Chloe, Theo, and Tadhg, for their patience while their mom was feeling the feelings and putting them to page. Pop-pop would have been so proud of the people you've become. Although he didn't live long enough to meet you, you're the living proof that the sacrifices he made were worth it. Finally, I want to thank my wife, Megan, for making this life — and this book — with me.

NOTES

Prologue

1. Fiona Apple, "Mix: Fiona Apple cover of The Whole of the Moon — Live version," https://www.youtube.com/watch?v=3dZ5KjFLxgA.

2. Mike Scott, "How We Made 'The Whole of the Moon,'" *Guardian*, July 27, 2020, https://www.theguardian.com/music/2020/jul/27/how-we-made-waterboys-the-whole-of-the-moon-mike-scott.

3. Fiona Apple, "Fiona Apple appreciates Sinéad O'Connor Mandinka," https://www.youtube.com/watch?v=rB3qDlu5Nvg.

4. Fiona Apple, "A Message to Sinéad O'Connor from Fiona Apple," https://www.youtube.com/watch?v=4ah51vQfRL8.

5. Sinéad O'Connor, 2017 Facebook video, https://www.youtube.com/watch?v=919ip9_urE0.

6. Its other name was Asylum Place, although my mother often just called it "Sout Philly" (you drop the "h"). For more, see Ken Finkel, "Saving (and Stretching) Devil's Pocket," Philly History Blog, October 28, 2014, https://blog.phillyhistory.org/index.php/2014/10/saving-and-stretching-devils-pocket.

7. In 2021, some members of Times Up's leadership came under fire amid accusations that they were complicit in an attempt to discredit and cover up sexual misconduct allegations against (now former) New York governor Andrew Cuomo. The movement has nevertheless drawn significant attention to sexual harassment in the workplace, particularly in the entertainment industry.

8. Allyson McCabe, "Sinéad O'Connor Has a New Memoir . . . And No Regrets," *NPR Morning Edition*, June 1, 2021, https://www.npr.org/2021/06/01/992501997/Sinéad-oconnor-has-a-new-memoir-and-no-regrets.

Framing

1. Sinéad O'Connor, *Saturday Night Live*, October 3, 1992, https://www.youtube.com/watch?v=XoVpfiMcPPA.

2. Joe Pesci, *Saturday Night Live*, October 10, 1992, https://www.youtube.com/watch?v=kPykO9jdLko.

3. Pesci's wiseguy character Vincent LaGuardia Gambini from the 1992 comedy film *My Cousin Vinny* was reprised in 1998, when he put out an album called *Vincent LaGuardia Gambini Sings Just for You*. It includes "Wise Guy," a misogynistic gangsta rap song in which Pesci brags, in

character, about how to treat "bitches," https://www.youtube.com/watch ?v=gqn3NhlqoeA.

4. There are a couple of pre-*SNL* Sinéad O'Connor biographies floating around, such as Jimmy Guterman's *Sinéad: Her Life and Music* (New York: Warner Books, 1991) and Dermott Hayes's *Sinéad O'Connor: So Different* (London: Omnibus Press, 1991).

5. "You wait years for a Sinéad O'Connor biography, then . . .," *Independent*, April 28, 2012, https://www.independent.ie/woman/celeb-news/you -wait-years-for-a-sinead-oconnor-biography-then-26848162.html.

6. Sinéad O'Connor, *Rememberings* (New York: HarperCollins, 2021).

7. O'Connor, *Rememberings*, 211.

Take I

1. Sinéad O'Connor, *Rememberings* (New York: HarperCollins, 2021), 18.

2. Sinéad O'Connor, "To Sinéad O'Connor, Pope Benedict's Apology for Church Sex Abuse Rings Hollow," *Washington Post*, March 28, 2010, https://www.washingtonpost.com/wp-dyn/content/article/2010/03/25 /AR2010032502363.html.

3. O'Connor, *Rememberings*, 28–29.

4. O'Connor has repeated her account of her mother's beatings many times, for example, in a 2001 interview with the *Independent*: "It was that kind of psychological destruction. On a regular basis I'd be made to take off my clothes and lie on the floor while she kicked me here [gestures towards genitals] and spit at it. And make me say things like 'I'm nothing,' and ask for mercy. There was a lot of sadism. The violence was sexually abusive."

5. You can see that scene here: https://www.youtube.com/watch?v= vML4fpOZrK8.

6. Karen Everhart, "Philly Gets its First Airing of 1968 Wiseman Film," *Current*, May 6, 2001, https://current.org/2001/05/philly-gets-its-first-airing -of-1968-wiseman-film/?wallit_nosession=1.

7. O'Connor, "To Sinéad O'Connor, Pope Benedict's Apology for Church Sex Abuse Rings Hollow."

8. Sinéad O'Connor, "An Open Letter from Sinéad O'Connor on the Magdalene Laundries Report," *Irish Post*, February 8, 2013, https://www.irishpost .com/news/an-open-letter-from-Sinéad-oconnor-on-the-magdalene -laundries-report-3212.

9. O'Connor, *Rememberings*, 61, and author conversation with O'Connor, May 15, 2021.

10. "Behind the Music: Sinéad O'Connor," *VH-1*, October 22, 2001.

11. Author conversation with O'Connor, May 15, 2021.

12. In Tua Nua timeline, http://www.intuanua.com/timeline.

13. A demo of In Tua Nua's "Take My Hand," https://www.youtube.com/watch?v=WBTEEZSV6sA.

14. O'Connor performing live with The Waterboys, circa 1984, https://www.youtube.com/watch?v=JOqqt9UoYU8.

15. This account appears in detail in Mikal Gilmore's "Sinéad O'Connor's Songs of Experience," in *Night Beat: A Shadow History of Rock & Roll* (New York: Random House, 1998), 312–330.

The Lion and the Cobra

1. *The Muppet Show*, season 5, episode 16, February 21, 1981, https://www.youtube.com/watch?v=lfPUCTQJnb8.

2. *The Muppet Show*, season 5, episode 16.

3. I've even interviewed her a couple of times, and she sang to me a little! Eleven-year-old me would have flipped out. Fifty-one-year-old me nearly cried.

4. In the liner notes for *The Lion and the Cobra*, O'Connor credits O'Ceallaigh with being "my biggest influence and my best friend."

5. Robert Hilburn, "From Rage to Reason: Sinéad O'Connor Burst onto the Scene in 1987 as an Odd-looking Provocateur. But Now, at 23, the Irish Singer-Songwriter has Matured into a Major Rock Force," *Los Angeles Times*, May 13, 1990, https://www.latimes.com/archives/la-xpm-1990-05-13-ca-402-story.html.

6. Sinéad O'Connor, *Rememberings* (New York: HarperCollins, 2021), 141.

7. Sinéad O'Connor at the 1989 Grammys, https://www.youtube.com/watch?v=fWY14l_HjDA.

8. Jeffrey Schiff, "Potter's Field," http://www.jeffreyschiff.net/homeleft/potters-field.

9. O'Connor, *Rememberings*, 147.

As Seen on MTV

1. This was a film still from the British black comedy *How I Won the War*, directed by Richard Lester (1967).

2. See a copy of *Rolling Stone*'s debut cover, https://worldcafe.tumblr.com/post/132887081291/in-1967-rock-and-roll-lovers-were-finally.

3. Charles Kaiser, "A Roach Clip with Every Paid Subscription," *New York Times*, June 17, 1990, https://www.nytimes.com/1990/06/17/books/a-roach-clip-with-every-paid-subscription.html.

4. Rob Tannenbaum and Craig Marks, *I Want My MTV: An Uncensored History of the Music Video Revolution* (New York: Plume, 2012).

5. David Weir, "Wenner's World: The evolution of Jann Wenner: How the

ultimate '6os rock groupie built his fantasy into a media empire." *Salon*, April 20, 1999, https://www.salon.com/1999/04/20/wenner.

6. Tannenbaum and Marks, *I Want My MTV*, 103. They describe the MTV team as "partying like college freshman," identifying Les Garland as "the biggest rock star on staff" who "knew everyone in the music biz yet still hung out with interns."

7. Jack Hamilton, "How Rock and Roll Became White," *Slate*, October 16, 2016, https://slate.com/culture/2016/10/race-rock-and-the-rolling -stones-how-the-rock-and-roll-became-white.html.

8. *Rolling Stone*'s Top 500 Songs, https://web.archive.org/web /20061228112332/http://www.rollingstone.com/news/story/6595852 /johnny_b_goode.

9. Jesse Wegman, "The Story of Chuck Berry's 'Maybellene,'" *NPR*, July 2, 2000, https://www.npr.org/2000/07/02/1076141/maybellene.

10. Although it must be noted that music videos were central to the marketing for the album.

11. For more on the historical context, see Christina Turner, "How Racism Pushed Tina Turner and other Black Women Artists out of America," *PBS News Hour Canvas*, April 21, 2021, https://www.pbs.org/newshour/arts /how-racism-pushed-tina-turner-and-other-black-women-artists-out-of -america.

12. Recordings are eligible a decade after their release.

13. Rock & Roll Hall of Fame, 2021, https://www.rockhall.com/inductees /tina-turner.

14. In 1985 the full spectrum of sound made by Black artists was not yet being heard, or recognized. To end this "musical apartheid," Living Colour guitarist Vernon Reid, journalist Greg Tate, Eye & I lead vocalist Dk Dyson, and producer Konda Mason founded the Black Rock Coalition, a New York–based nonprofit collective that identified recording and performance spaces and distribution opportunities, designed album covers to call attention to the music inside rather than the race of the artists who made it, and established an educational wing to reclaim rock's Black roots through exhibitions and events. Steve Hochman, "Black Rock Coalition Pushes for an End to 'Musical Apartheid,'" *Los Angeles Times*, June 14, 1989.

15. Inspired by the success of "We are the World," Van Zandt wrote a song that pledged the boycott of Sun City, a South African luxury resort and casino that had long lured white artists from the United States and England with huge financial incentives. As Van Zandt started recruiting artists to participate in recording the song and concurrent behind-the-scenes documentary project, Bruce Springsteen and Miles Davis were early signees. The final lineup for "Sun City" also included Afrika Bambaataa, Ray Barretto, Stiv Bators, Pat Benatar, Kurtis Blow, Bono, Jackson Browne, Ron

Carter, Clarence Clemons, Jimmy Cliff, George Clinton, Bob Dylan, The Fat Boys, Peter Gabriel, Peter Garrett, Bob Geldof, Lotti Golden, Hall & Oates, Daryl Hannah, Herbie Hancock, Nona Hendryx, Kashif, DJ Kool Herc, Eddie Kendricks, Darlene Love, Grandmaster Melle Mel, Michael Monroe, Bonnie Raitt, Joey Ramone, Lou Reed, Keith Richards, David Ruffin, Run-D.M.C., Gil Scott-Heron, Lakshminarayana Shankar, Ringo Starr, Peter Wolf, Bobby Womack, Ronnie Wood, Big Youth, and others.

16. Chris Jordan, "The Industry Didn't Want Hip-Hop on the 'Sun City' Record Says Little Steven Van Zandt," *Asbury Park Press*, August 12, 2021, https://www.app.com/story/entertainment/music/2021/08/12/little-steven-van-zandt-sun-city-hip-hop-rap-rappers-south-africa/8113803002.

Rock-'n'-Roll Cassandra

1. David Bowie gets a lot of credit for this confrontation. Over the years he has had many Black collaborators and has consistently spoken out against racism. However, it should also be noted that Rock Against Racism (RAR) was formed in the United Kingdom in the 1970s as a direct response to profascist comments Bowie made in several publications, which he later attributed to an interest in the occult, Nietzsche, and drug use. Eric Clapton had also made racist and anti-immigrant statements on several occasions, even though Black blues music was foundational to his repertoire.

2. Gail Mitchell, "Exclusive: How Michael Jackson's 'Thriller' Changed the Music Business," *Billboard*, July 3, 2009, https://www.billboard.com/music/music-news/exclusive-how-michael-jacksons-thriller-changed-the-music-business-268212.

3. In 1975, the renamed Jacksons left Motown for Epic Records, a unit of CBS, which gave them more creative freedom and higher royalty rates.

4. Jackson's then-publicist, Norman Winter, tried to arrange a cover but was told by Wenner in a letter dated November 27, 1979, that "[w]e would very much like to do a major piece on Michael Jackson, but feel it is not a cover story." Jackson's handwritten response has circulated widely on the internet.

5. Emily Votaw, "Duets Featuring Michael Jackson, Freddie Mercury to be Released," *Billboard*, July 29, 2013, https://www.billboard.com/music/music-news/duets-featuring-michael-jackson-freddie-mercury-to-be-released-5046772.

6. Hear an early demo of "Beat It," https://www.youtube.com/watch?v=eZeYw1bm53Y.

7. The whole thing about the monitor speakers catching on fire is restated here at about 7:05, https://www.youtube.com/watch?v=e-H1mCEA0iA#t=7m00s.

8. At that time, it wasn't widely known that Eddie Van Halen was of Dutch and Indonesian descent. In his later years, he would speak often about the racism he encountered growing up, https://www.nbcnews.com/news/asian-america/eddie-van-halen-endured-horrifying-racist-environment-becoming-rock-legend-n1242663.

9. Across the board, MTV's strategy was to project the appearance of fresh programming while "narrowcasting"; in other words, the network tailored the content to target a specific advertising demographic.

10. Rob Tannenbaum and Craig Marks, *I Want My MTV: An Uncensored History of the Music Video Revolution* (New York: Plume, 2012).

11. As MTV superseded radio as a promotional outlet, new recording contracts were increasingly written with video production clauses. In-demand directors could command upwards of six-figure fees for their work.

12. Eddie Van Halen later had no qualms about taking credit for his work on "Beat It." Mick Jagger became interested in working with Jackson and they re-recorded one of the Freddie Mercury demos, "State of Shock," as a duet appearing on the Jacksons' 1984 *Victory* album, reaching number fourteen on the US singles chart.

13. Tannenbaum and Marks, *I Want My MTV*.

14. Barry Walters, "Rick Rubin: The King of Rap," *Village Voice*, November 4, 1986, https://www.villagevoice.com/2020/02/27/rick-rubin-the-king-of-rap.

15. Formed in response to what they saw as the Beasties' promotion of rape culture, the short-lived Berkeley-based feminist rap trio the Yeastie Girlz released a 1988 7-inch called Ovary Action, https://www.youtube.com/watch?v=pFayUOMXhxU.

16. Alan Light, "The Story of Yo: The Oral History of the Beastie Boys," *SPIN*, September 4, 1998, https://www.spin.com/1998/09/story-yo-oral-history-beastie-boys/2.

17. Whitney Houston Reminisces About 80's Music on MTV, https://www.youtube.com/watch?v=IzZgor4981M.

18. You can see that video here, https://www.youtube.com/watch?v=PCe03R546r4.

19. In Madonna's case, it was "nothing to worry about here folks, she's only 'Like A Virgin.'" In Lauper's case, it was the nonthreatening idea that "Girls Just Wanna Have Fun."

20. Even though Annie Lennox's self-presentation scrambled gender codes, she was clear and consistent in her interviews that her androgynous look was motivated by the desire to be seen on equal footing with men, and not a statement about her offstage gender or sexual identity, which was cis and straight.

21. Marjorie Williams, "MTV's Short Takes Define a New Style," *Washington*

Post, December 13, 1989, https://www.washingtonpost.com/archive/politics/1989/12/13/mtvs-short-takes-define-a-new-style/b2134283-89a3-47fb-877d-2fba60da4239.

22. MTV promo interview for *The Lion and the Cobra*, https://www.youtube.com/watch?v=jl9Tjlq-9GA.

23. After expressing admiration for sixteen-year-old rapper MC Lyte's 1987 single "I Cram to Understand U (Sam)," O'Connor enlisted Lyte to collaborate on a remix of "I Want Your (Hands on Me)," and a music video, which debuted on MTV in May 1988. That same month Lyte broke through the male-dominated world of rap to become the first female rapper to release a solo album, *Lyte as a Rock*. Lyte went on to release eight albums and earn a lifetime achievement award from BET in 2013.

24. Interview in Toronto, November 1987, https://www.youtube.com/watch?v=MkeaUT1tvN8.

25. Sinéad O'Connor, *Rememberings* (New York: HarperCollins, 2021), 204.

26. Marcelle Clements, "Sinead O'Connor, Uncensored," *Esquire*, 1991, https://www.esquire.com/entertainment/music/a36098266/sinead-oconnor-1991-profile-interview.

27. The concept of intersectionality, coined in 1989 by Kimberle Crenshaw, was not yet widely known or understood outside of academic circles.

28. Robert Hilburn, "Sinead O'Connor Has Got It," *Los Angeles Times*, May 31, 1990, https://www.latimes.com/archives/la-xpm-1990-05-31-ca-660-story.html.

29. Anthony DeCurtis, "The Lion and the Cobra," *Rolling Stone*, January 28, 1988, https://www.rollingstone.com/music/music-album-reviews/the-lion-and-the-cobra-252050.

30. Jon Pareles, "Out on a Limb, Shouting," *New York Times*, January 31, 1988, https://timesmachine.nytimes.com/timesmachine/1988/01/31/315588.html?pageNumber=258.

*SPIN*ning Sinéad

1. As a notable exception, Guccione Jr. had a long-running beef with Axl Rose of Guns N' Roses, who called him out in "Get in the Ring." It goes, "Bob Guccione Jr. at Spin/What? You pissed off cuz your dad gets more pussy than you?/Fuck you/Suck my fuckin' dick . . . /Get in the ring motherfucker/And I'll kick your bitchy little ass/Punk."

2. See, for example, Kim Gordon, "Big and Bouncy," *SPIN*, September 1989, https://books.google.com/books?id=PK1uLUXpAzoC&lpg=PA50&ots=aH6_oJ7V-x&dq=SPIN%20magazine%20%22ll%20cool%20j%22%20gordon&pg=PA50#v=onepage&q&f=false. Gordon has publicly reflected on her experience several times, including in John Blanco, "Stay-

ing Kool: Sonic Youth Survives a Major Label," *Phoenix New Times*, March 20, 1991, http://www.phoenixnewtimes.com/music/staying-koolsonic -youth-survives-a-major-label-6412020; and in her memoir *Girl in A Band* (New York: Dey St./William Morrow, 2015). See also bell hooks's interview with Ice Cube, *SPIN*, April 1993, https://books.google.com/bo oks?id=gxsArQZdyBwC&pg=PA79&lpg=PA79&dq=spin+ice+cube +bell+hooks&source=bl&ots=OoHpHr3thK&sig=ACfU3UoEkPJ-Fr kVf66pJHvgKPWysA7oCw&hl=en&sa=X&ved=2ahUKEwjfyZuvuu H1AhUKkokEHaPUDkQQ6AF6BAgYEAM#v=onepage&q=spin%20 ice%20cube%20bell%20hooks&f=false. hooks talks about the experience here, bell hooks, "Sexism and Misogyny: Who Takes the Rap?" http:// challengingmalesupremacy.org/wp-content/uploads/2015/04/Misogyny -gangsta-rap-and-The-Piano-bell-hooks.pdf.

3.   Guccione Jr. described Kiersh as "a brilliant investigative journalist," though he's primarily known for his writing about collectibles such as coins, stamps, cameras, pens, and golf. For the *Daily Beast* reprint of the *SPIN* story, see "Ike Turner: Why I Beat Tina," *SPIN*, July 13, 2015, https://www.thedailybeast.com/ike-turner-why-i-beat-tina.

4.   Richard Harrington. "The Medium is the Mayhem," *Washington Post*, May 13, 1990, https://www.washingtonpost.com/archive/lifestyle/style /1990/05/13/the-medium-is-the-mayhem/72a4e924-517c-4716-b311 -5d7647dd81e4.

5.   "Rock 'n' roll is sex is rock 'n' roll," Kuipers explained. Only one month after the *SPIN* story came out, bassist Flea and drummer Chad Smith were arrested in Florida on charges of leaping from the stage and attempting to sexually assault a woman in the audience. "Two Members of Red Hot Chili Peppers Arrested," *UPI Archives*, March 17, 1990, https://www.upi .com/Archives/1990/03/17/Two-members-of-Red-Hot-Chili-Peppers -arrested/7434637650000.

6.   Hazel Cills, "*SPIN* Re-hires Founder Who Created Hostile Work Environment for Women," *Jezebel*, May 15, 2020, https://jezebel.com/spin -magazine-brings-back-founder-who-created-hostile-e-1843479360.

7.   Thomas S. Mulligan, "Workers Tell of Harassment at *SPIN*," *Los Angeles Times*, March 21, 1997, https://www.latimes.com/archives/la-xpm-1997 -03-21-fi-40617-story.html.

8.   Lauren Spencer, "It Happened to Me." *Jane*, September/October 1997.

9.   When I interviewed Spencer on September 5, 2022, she stood by all the details in the *Jane* story and filled in these as well.

10.   Bob Guccione Jr., "Sinéad O'Connor: *SPIN*'s 1991 Cover Story, 'Special Child,'" *SPIN*, September 18, 2015, https://www.spin.com/2015/09 /sinead-oconnor-interview-spin-30-cover-story.

11.   Author interview, September 7, 2022.

12. According to Wilder, the column had been carved out from a much larger and more substantive interview, and she expressed deep regret for the version that *SPIN* published. Wilder says that when she met with O'Connor in late 1987, she found O'Connor to be "very much her own person," recalling that O'Connor spoke candidly about how she had been mistreated by men in the industry and the media, noting that they seemed fixated on her breasts rather than her music (a position supported by *SPIN*'s choice of photo).

     Wilder says that she found O'Connor to be serious and sincere, and that much of their conversation focused on matters of race. Though American slavery and the civil rights movement were not typically taught in European schools, Wilder says that O'Connor spoke about learning about these subjects on her own. She says O'Connor expressed admiration for the resilience and nobility of Black people who found the strength and spirit to survive through song—which she said she related to because of her own experience of music. When Wilder submitted her draft to *SPIN*, she says they rejected it immediately, pulling in only what fit their narrative. Author interview, August 31, 2022.

13. In April 1989, "Mandinka" also came in at number seventy-six on its "greatest singles" list. For *Billboard*'s chart history for *The Lion and the Cobra*, see https://www.billboard.com/artist/sinead-oconnor/chart-history/tlp.

14. Legs McNeil, "Sinéad O'Connor: A Captivating Contradiction," *SPIN*, April 1990.

15. Celia Farber, "The Trial," *Salon*, June 9, 1997, https://www.salon.com/1997/06/09/spin970609.

16. A notable exception is *Rolling Stone*'s Mikal Gilmore, who portrays O'Connor as an artist and a person who deserves being taken seriously and compares her to other truth-telling singer-songwriters, such as Van Morrison, Lou Reed, and Leonard Cohen. While Gilmore goes into O'Connor's past, explicitly referencing the abuse she suffered, he's careful to show how she channeled her experiences into her music without suggesting that she or her art are defined by it. In his review of *I Do Not Want What I Haven't Got*, Gilmore says the album "is less about O'Connor's ambitions than the cost of those ambitions." Mikal Gilmore, "I Do Not Want What I Haven't Got," *Rolling Stone*, January 22, 1997, https://www.rollingstone.com/music/music-album-reviews/i-do-not-want-what-i-havent-got-94290.

17. Sheila Rogers, "Face to Face with Fame," *Rolling Stone*, October 4, 1990.

She'll Talk but You Won't Listen

1. Sinéad O'Connor, *Rememberings* (New York: HarperCollins, 2021), 139.
2. Hilton Als, "Sinéad O'Connor: The Irish Firebrand Heats it Up All Over Again," *Interview*, https://www.members.tripod.com/dcebe/int_sep02.txt.
3. Als, "Sinéad O'Connor."
4. Rather than intending to "censor" Clay, O'Connor tried to explain her motives to the *Los Angeles Times*, reasoning that "it would be nonsensical of 'Saturday Night Live' to expect a woman to perform songs about a woman's experience after a monologue by Andrew Dice Clay. I feel it shows disrespect to women that 'Saturday Night Live' expected me to perform on the same show as Andrew Dice Clay." See Robert Hilburn, "Nothing Compares 2 Her Year," *Los Angeles Times*, December 16, 1990, https://www.latimes.com/archives/la-xpm-1990-12-16-ca-9231-story.html.
5. "Listeners Angered by Sinéad O'Connor," *Washington Post*, August 27,1990, https://www.washingtonpost.com/archive/lifestyle/1990/08/28/listeners-angered-by-sinead-oconnor/b0b89b89-3ec1-4ad8-8978-4dd80513f342.
6. O'Connor appeared in disguise with a friend to laugh at the protesters who gathered outside of New York's Saratoga Performing Arts Center at the height of "The Star-Spangled Banner" controversy.
7. "Disc Jockey Reinstated After Attack on Singer," *Buffalo News*, September 6, 1990, https://buffalonews.com/news/disc-jockey-reinstated-after-attack-on-singer/article_2a29d792-3239-509c-b8cb-18a808028c9.html.
8. Tracy Wilkinson, "Clerk at Upscale Grocery Strikes Sour Note With Singer," *Los Angeles Times*, October 6, 1990, https://www.latimes.com/archives/la-xpm-1990-10-06-mn-1612-story.html.

The Takedown

1. In October of that year, a jury found the group not guilty of obscenity charges on appeal, but in between a Broward County sheriff arrested record-store owner George Freeman on obscenity charges for selling the album.
2. MTV Kurt Loder interview with Sinéad O'Connor, https://www.youtube.com/watch?v=KwvMPpWYKJc.
3. Dennis Hunt, "MTV: The Naughty Envelope, Please," *Los Angeles Times*, September 8, 1990, https://www.latimes.com/archives/la-xpm-1990-09-08-ca-599-story.html.
4. Eric Snider, "This Time O'Connor's Message Was Clear." *Tampa Bay Times*, September 8. 1990, https://www.tampabay.com/archive/1990/09/08/this-time-o-connor-s-message-was-clearer.

5. Billboard Music Awards, 1990, https://www.youtube.com/watch?v=rS2PNOlc2QE.

6. Sheila Rogers, "Face to Face with Fame," *Rolling Stone*, October 4, 1990.

7. Sinéad O'Connor, *Rememberings* (New York: HarperCollins, 2021), 153–162.

8. Around this time, O'Connor appeared in a primetime TV interview with Maria Shriver where the film crew focused on her boots and Shriver lobbed inane questions. "One day you decided to shave your head . . ." she began. When O'Connor nodded, Shriver continued, "Well, how did you think it looked?" O'Connor just shrugged and quietly replied, "Fine." Nobody said a word about Shriver, but O'Connor was widely criticized for being uncommunicative. "O'Connor's appearance on 'The Cutting Edge with Maria Shriver,'" https://www.youtube.com/watch?v=wlC_VE-G7bY.

9. Robert Hilburn, "Nothing Compares 2 Her Year," *Los Angeles Times*, December 16, 1990.

10. Arsenio Hall first appearance, 1991, part 1, https://www.youtube.com/watch?v=eIoPAaZGUiA, and part 2, https://www.youtube.com/watch?v=TcnQ4KUBDj8.

11. McNeil opines that earlier that year "she looked more like a 12-year-old who'd skipped school and broken into the hotel [where their interview took place]." Legs McNeil, Artist of the Year interview, *SPIN*, December 1990.

12. Frank Newport, "In U.S., 87% Approve of Black-White Marriage, vs. 4% in 1958," *Gallup*, https://news.gallup.com/poll/163697/approve-marriage-blacks-whites.aspx.

13. Arsenio Hall, second appearance, 1991, https://www.youtube.com/watch?v=mAf7fGEeRQs.

14. O'Connor mentions the event, but she does not name Hall in *Rememberings*, 150. However, she did publicly name Hall in 2016, at the same time she accused him of being Prince's drug dealer. See Georgia McCafferty, "Arsenio Hall Sues 'Attention Seeker' Sinéad O'Connor," *CNN*, May 6, 2016, https://www.cnn.com/2016/05/06/entertainment/arsenio-hall-sinead-oconnor.

Is She Not Your Girl?

1. Bob Guccione Jr., "Special Child," *SPIN*, November 1991.

2. Sandra Bernhard on Arsenio, 1991, https://www.youtube.com/watch?v=-cWXiRifPEw.

3. David Wild, "Sinéad O'Connor: The Rolling Stone Interview," *Rolling Stone*, March 7, 1991, https://www.rollingstone.com/music/music-features/sinead-oconnor-the-rolling-stone-interview-181665.

4. Elyse Gardner, "Am I Not Your Girl?" *Rolling Stone*, November 26, 1992, https://www.rollingstone.com/music/music-album-reviews/am-i-not -your-girl-187171.

5. Robert Christgau, https://www.robertchristgau.com/get_album.php?id= 6067.

6. Sinéad O'Connor, "Success Has Made a Failure of Our Home," https:// www.youtube.com/watch?v=T2EiVnOm2aE. Here is an interview with O'Connor the day after *SNL*, "Sinead O'Connor Talks About Ripping Picture of the Pope on SNL—(The Day After)," October 7, 2014, https:// www.youtube.com/watch?v=6P0NwE9Xa2k.

This Means War

1. Today each episode of *SNL* draws somewhere around 5 million viewers.

2. Megan Rosenfeld, "Sinéad's Perplexing Protest," *Washington Post*, October 6, 1992, https://www.washingtonpost.com/archive/lifestyle/1992/10 /06/sineads-perplexing-protest/71e84b15-36fa-4778-946f-a17706b6511a.

3. Rosenfeld, "Sinéad's Perplexing Protest."

4. Gordon Oliver, "Sex Abuse Sparks Program" *National Catholic Reporter*, September 23, 1983, http://www.natcath.org/crisis/092383.htm.

5. William M. Reilly, "Steamroller crushes Sinead O'Connor recordings," *UPI*, October 21, 1992, https://www.upi.com/Archives/1992/10/21 /Steamroller-crushes-Sinéad-OConnor-recordings/5284719640000.

6. O'Connor's appearance on *SNL* was even mocked on *SNL*. Jan Hooks hosted "The Sinéad O'Connor Goodtime Happy Jamboree," a skit featuring leprechauns and Irish folk music, which gets interrupted by boos, resulting in Hooks leaving the stage. Hooks later reappears in the episode, this time explaining that she thought it was Hitler in the photo she destroyed, not the pope. The audience boos again, causing her to lose her composure. Adam Sandler shouts from the audience, "We don't want you to hate! We want you to love others!"

7. Madonna's ambition was "to rule the world" as she famously told Dick Clark when she appeared on *American Bandstand* in 1983, https://www .youtube.com/watch?v=orwhstP7DIU. More on Madonna's acolytes, "MTV—Madonna—Blond Date Weekend—Report on Madonna Wan- nabe—Madonnaland—1985," https://youtu.be/2NAqWpd3TbU.

8. Just as the media had manufactured Madonna's rivalry with Cyndi Lauper, it cooked up a new rivalry with O'Connor. But only one side was willing to step into the ring.

9. "Madonna Says Sinéad Went Too Far," *Buffalo News*, October 19, 1992, https://buffalonews.com/news/madonna-says-Sinéad-went-too-far /article_a62511d4-cd9b-5992-8fb1-cb9de4ffa7d2.html.

10. Robert Christgau, "Folkie Madonna," https://www.robertchristgau.com /xg/rock/Sinéad-90.php.

11. Jon Pareles, "Why Sinéad O'Connor Hit a Nerve," *New York Times*, November 1, 1992, https://www.nytimes.com/1992/11/01/arts/pop-view -why-Sinéad-o-connor-hit-a-nerve.html.

12. New York's Cardinal John O'Connor (no relation to Sinéad) was also well known as a symbol of the Church's intolerance, his face appearing on a popular ACT-UP poster, where he was tagged a public health menace. For all of his hospital visits with AIDS patients, O'Connor actively opposed HIV/AIDS education and aggressively fought broader LGBTQ anti-discrimination efforts. Although the Church's child abuse scandal was only beginning to surface in the mainstream American media, none of us would have been surprised to learn, as we did years later, that Cardinal O'Connor was also busy covering up for Archbishop Theodore McCarrick, one of the most egregious sexual abusers of boys and seminarians.

13. Sinéad O'Connor, *Rememberings* (New York: HarperCollins, 2021), 178. She actually misremembers the details a bit in her memoir, relaying that it was Geldof tearing up the photo of John Travolta and Olivia Newton-John. You can see the appearance here, https://www.youtube.com/watch?v= hmm—HkLjIg.

14. O'Connor, *Rememberings*, 177.

15. O'Connor saw immediate parallels between the English colonization of Jamaica and Ireland, but whereas Irish Catholicism emphasized a God who was far away and largely unattainable, Rastafarian music spoke of God's presence and protective watchfulness.

16. Stephen Holden, "Madonna Makes $60 Million Deal," *New York Times*, April 20, 1992, https://www.nytimes.com/1992/04/20/arts/madonna -makes-a-60-million-deal.html.

We Do Not Want What She Has Got

1. Sinéad O'Connor, *Rememberings* (New York: HarperCollins, 2021), 181.

2. O'Connor, *Rememberings*, 215.

3. She had previously expressed sympathy for the IRA, and for Mike Tyson, who had recently been charged with rape, telling *Rolling Stone*'s Alan Light that she thought his accuser was "a bitch who used him." Alan Light, "Sinéad O'Connor Speaks," *Rolling Stone*, October 29, 1992.

4. William Leith, "The Life of Saint Sinéad," *Independent*, November 29, 1992.

5. Megan Rosenfeld, "Sinéad's Perplexing Protest," *Washington Post*, October 6, 1992, https://www.washingtonpost.com/archive/lifestyle/1992/10 /06/Sinéads-perplexing-protest/71e84b15-36fa-4778-946f-a17706b6511a.

6. Guccione Jr. sold *SPIN* in 1997 for $43.5 million.

7. Len Righi, "Legs McNeil Tries to Strike a Nerve with New Rock-'n'-Roll Magazine," *McCalls*, April 18, 1993, https://www.mcall.com/news/mc-xpm-1993-04-18-2922722-story.html. McNeil claimed that *Nerve* had a starting circulation of 100,000 subscribers in addition to being sold at 37,000 newsstands nationwide. Although the magazine folded a year into its print run, McNeil continued to peddle in smut. One of his next projects was co-writing porn star Marylin Chambers's 1999 comeback *Still Insatiable*.

8. Geoff Edgers, "Sinéad O'Connor is still in one piece," *Washington Post*, March 18, 2020, https://www.washingtonpost.com/graphics/2020/entertainment/Sinéad-oconnor-still-in-one-piece.

9. Maggie O'Kane, "'I fit in here,' Sinéad O'Connor says of her return to Dublin," *Guardian*. May 3, 1993.

10. O'Connor, *Rememberings*, 211.

11. Matthew Gilbert, "Sinéad O'Connor on child abuse, suicide, and Kurt Cobain," *Baltimore Sun*, September 4, 1994, https://www.baltimoresun.com/news/bs-xpm-1994-09-04-1994247194-story.html.

12. Stephanie Zacharek, "Universal Mother," *Rolling Stone*, October 6, 1994, https://www.rollingstone.com/music/music-album-reviews/universal-mother-193409.

13. Bill Graham, "Universal Mother," *Hot Press*, April 9, 2001, https://www.hotpress.com/music/universal-mother-482593.

14. Michael Azerrad, *Come As You Are: The Story of Nirvana* (New York: Doubleday, 1994), 32.

15. The release of "Famine" came at a time of deep tension between Ireland and England. A TV show in London tried to dissuade her from performing it because it was "too political." Unsurprisingly, O'Connor pushed back. There's a YouTube video of her appearing on *Later with Jools Holland*, https://www.youtube.com/watch?v=-Ogwwlzm5vc.

16. "Sinéad O'Connor Signs with Atlantic," *Billboard*, July 7, 1998.

17. Chris Norris, "Sinéad O'Connor Starts Anew," *Billboard*, July 11, 1998, and "Sinéad O'Connor: Not a Bastard Anymore," *SPIN*, August 1998, 112.

18. In England, Mother's Day is celebrated in March.

19. Neil Michael, "Sinéad Was So Sick and Frightened but She Will Never Give Up Her Fight for the Daughter She Adores," *Mirror*, April 9, 1999, https://www.thefreelibrary.com/%27Sinead+was+so+sick+and+frightened%2C+but+she+will+never+give+up+her...-a060389339.

20. It has been widely misreported that O'Connor appeared on the show before her meeting with Cox and subsequent ordination. In fact, she was ordained on April 22, 1999, and then appeared on the show on April 30. She told Byrne, "What I call my holy trinity is I am mother, I am a singer

and I am a priest, these things are equally sacred to me." See https://www
.rte.ie/archives/2019/0329/1039381-female-priest-sinead-oconnor.

21. Note that as far back as 1990, O'Connor was performing in a white hooded robe that resembled a nun's habit. See Robert Hilburn, "Nothing Compares 2 Her Year," *Los Angeles Times*, December 16, 1990.

22. "Sinéad O'Connor on Queen Latifah, Part 2," https://www.youtube.com /watch?v=maS8GxRGa-0, and Ian Ransom, *Waiting for the Rapture: Scenes from a Magical Life* (iUniverse, 2006), 121.

23. *Curve* Interview, June 8, 2000, https://www.curvemag.com/blog /interviews/curves-20th-anniversary-retrospective-sinad-oconnor.

24. At the time, Cesares was such a sensation that she garnered her own profile in *New York Magazine*. Jonathan Van Meter, "Who's That Girl?" *New York Magazine*, July 27, 1998, https://nymag.com/nymetro/news/people /features/3347.

25. Then in a letter sent to the *Hot Press* on June 8, 2000, she reportedly wrote, "I am a lesbian. I love men, but I prefer sex with women, and I prefer romantic relationships with women." See also "Sinéad Comes out of the *Hot Press*," *Independent*, June 11, 2000, https://www.independent.ie/irish -news/Sinéad-comes-out-of-the-hot-press-26255019.html.

26. Donna Freydkin, "Lilith Fair: Lovely, Lively and Long Overdue," CNN, July 28, 1998, http://www.cnn.com/SHOWBIZ/Music/9807/28/lilith .fair.

27. "O'Connor leaves Atlantic," *Billboard*, November 30, 2001, https://www .billboard.com/music/music-news/stewart-baker-oconnor-latest-to -leave-atlantic-77571.

28. "A sentimental indulgence destined for a theme-pub half-life," *Uncut*, November 2002, 114.

29. Jake Tapper, "Sin," *Salon*, October 12, 2002, https://www.salon.com/2002 /10/12/sinead_3.

30. Debbie Elliot, "Sinéad O'Connor Finds New Roots in Jamaica," *All Things Considered*, October 16, 2005, https://www.npr.org/2005/10/16/4961027 /sinead-oconnor-finds-new-roots-in-jamaica.

31. "Say a Little Prayer," *London Mirror*, June 8, 2007, https://www.mirror.co .uk/lifestyle/going-out/music/say-a-little-prayer-480702.

Wrecking Ball

1. At the time, Dr. Phil's show was consistently ranked among the highest-rated talk shows, with roughly 6 million viewers tuning in each week.

2. Sinéad O'Connor, "I Want a Man," *Independent*, August 21, 2011, https://www.independent.ie/woman/celeb-news/article2853772.ece #ixzz1ViBogdLU.

Notes to Pages 142-155

3. Ravi Somaiya, "Sinéad O'Connor's 'How About I Be Me (and You be You)?'" *New York Times*, February 10, 2012, https://www.nytimes.com/2012/02/12/arts/music/Sinéad-oconnors-how-about-i-be-me-and-you-be-you.html.

4. Will Hermes, "How About I Be Me (and You Be You)?" *Rolling Stone*, February 21, 2012, https://www.rollingstone.com/music/music-album-reviews/how-about-i-be-me-and-you-be-you-188354.

5. Dave Simpson, "How About I Be Me (and You Be You)?" *Guardian*, March 1, 2012, https://www.theguardian.com/music/2012/mar/01/Sinéad-oconnor-how-about-review.

6. "Sinéad O'Connor Dons Unflattering Stomach-Baring Outfit for Irish Performance," *Daily Mail*, August 11, 2011, https://www.dailymail.co.uk/tvshowbiz/article-2023903/Sinead-OConnor-unrecognisable-dons-unflattering-stomach-baring-outfit-Irish-performance.html.

7. Josh Eells, "Miley Cyrus: Confessions of Pop's Wildest Child," *Rolling Stone*, September 24, 2013, https://www.rollingstone.com/music/music-news/miley-cyrus-confessions-of-pops-wildest-child-115353.

8. Author conversation with O'Connor, May 15, 2021.

9. Miley Cyrus interview on *Today*, https://www.youtube.com/watch?v=XvL4MhogCxc.

10. O'Connor responding to Cyrus on RTÉ, https://www.youtube.com/watch?v=WUCmAkow4lo.

Things Need to Change

1. Sean Michaels, "Prince: I was born epileptic," *Guardian*, April 29, 2009, https://www.theguardian.com/music/2009/apr/29/prince-born-epileptic.

2. Richard Corliss, "The Prom Queen of Soul," *Time*, July 13, 1987, https://content.time.com/time/subscriber/article/0,33009,964980-1,00.html. Note that Corliss leads with a description of Houston as "Miss Black America" and remarks that she looks like "a Cosby kid made in heaven." Her singing ability comes later, almost as a surprise.

3. See also Houston's Gospel-inspired 4/4 performance of "The National Anthem" at the 1991 Superbowl, analyzed at length in Gerrick Kennedy, *Didn't We Almost Have It All: In Defense of Whitney Houston* (New York: Abrams Press, 2022), 147-172.

4. Robyn Crawford, *A Song for You: My Life with Whitney Houston* (New York: Dutton, 2019).

5. Madonna's unedited 2016 *Billboard* speech, https://www.youtube.com/watch?v=2H4giIAze48.

6. Part of this change has been made possible by the fragmentation of the

music industry. Traditional attention-getting events just don't hold the same sway with the public as they used to. No one is buying magazines or tuning in to network or cable TV to see which stars are on top and which are about to break through. As a striking example, in 2021, Grammy ratings hit an all-time low, with only 8.8 million viewers, down more than 50 percent from the year before. Compare that to decades ago, for example, in 1984 when 51.67 million people watched Michael Jackson take home eight trophies for *Thriller*.

7. Although the economics of independent and DIY music-making need to be worked out, artists now have alternative ways to produce music and distribute it themselves, establishing their own promotional platforms and mechanisms for engaging with fans, and deciding how they want to align their interests individually and collectively.

8. Kesha, Lady Gaga, and Mariah Carey are among those who have talked openly about being physically, sexually, and emotionally abused by former producers. Tori Amos, Beyoncé, P!nk, and Fiona Apple have transformed traumatic experiences into art.

9. Whereas three decades ago O'Connor's exposure of racial discrimination at the Grammys made her the subject of media hit jobs, it is now widely recognized, and artists such as Drake and the Weeknd have called out the Recording Academy's empty promises of change. The media has also started to address the Recording Academy's historical gender imbalance, no longer toeing former President Neil Portnow's line that women simply need to "step up." When the Recording Academy fired CEO Deborah Duggan in 2020, the media spotlight centered on a detailed letter she wrote to the Academy's human resources office immediately before her ouster, rather than focusing solely on the ouster itself. (Only five months into her tenure, Duggan had brought forward credible personal allegations of sexual harassment and affirmed the validity of long-standing complaints about lack of transparency, conflicts of interest, and the failure to recognize the achievements of female and BIPOC artists.)

We Need to Talk about Prince

1. Joe Taysom, "Revisiting the shocking moment Prince was booed off the Rolling Stones' stage," *Far Out*, May 25, 2020, https://faroutmagazine.co.uk/prince-booed-off-stage-supporting-the-rolling-stones.

2. Alan Light, *Let's Go Crazy: Prince and the Making of Purple Rain* (New York: Atria Books, 2014).

3. Pauline Kael, "Purple Rain," *New Yorker*, August 20, 1984, https://scrapsfromtheloft.com/movies/purple-rain-pauline-kael.

4. Vincent Canby, "Purple Rain, With Prince," *New York Times*, July 27, 1984,

https://www.nytimes.com/1984/07/27/movies/purple-rain-with-prince
.html.

5. Among the collaborators Prince is also said to have dated are Sheila E.,
   Sheena Easton, Carmen Electra, Anna "Fantastic" Garcia, Mayte Garcia,
   Jill Jones, Madonna, Susannah Melvoin, Susan Moonsie, and Vanity.
   Among those who were underage when they met are Anna "Fantastic"
   Garcia, Mayte Garcia, and Susan Moonsie. Prince's rumored involvement
   with teenage girls puts him in company with David Bowie, Elvis, Marvin
   Gaye, Mick Jagger, R. Kelly, Jerry Lee Lewis, Ted Nugent, Jimmy Page,
   Iggy Pop, Johnny Thunders, Tyga, Steven Tyler, and Bill Wyman.

6. Prince's female collaborators include Linda Anderson, The Bangles, Lisa
   Coleman, Gayle Chapman, Misty Copeland, Sheila E., Sheena Easton,
   Carmen Electra, Anna "Fantastic" Garcia, Mayte Garcia, Cat Glover,
   Donna Gratis, Jill Jones, Chaka Khan, Apollonia Kotero, Lianne La Havas,
   Cyndi Lauper, Madonna, Martika, Denise "Vanity" Matthews, Wendy
   Melvoin, Susannah Melvoin, Susan Moonsie, Stevie Nicks, Ida Kristine
   Nielsen, Patrice Rushen, Taja Sevelle, Mavis Staples, Bria Valente, Hannah
   Welton, and Red Wood. His longtime engineer, Susan Rogers, was said to
   be the only person he allowed in the room when he was recording, a sign
   of his trust in her skills and judgment.

7. Many of the accusations appear in tabloids or blogs, which is problematic
   since they presumably haven't been rigorously investigated and verified.
   However, it's also important to note that these are the same kinds of
   sources where similar reporting on women has often been accepted as
   fact. Ryan Parker, "Baby, I've got this thing for you," *Daily Mail*, April 26,
   2016, https://www.dailymail.co.uk/news/article-3558516/Baby-ve-got
   -thing-want-communicate-tonight-minds-Chauffeur-tells-Sheena-Easton
   -flipped-Prince-gave-silent-treatment-date.html.

8. Charlene Friend quoted in Nilufer Atik, "Prince made me call him
   Messiah," *Evening Standard/Daily Mail*, https://www.dailymail.co.uk
   /tvshowbiz/article-181815/Prince-Messiah.html.

9. Jill Jones, "The Confidences of Jill Jones," *Lipstick Alley*, June 11, 2019,
   https://www.lipstickalley.com/threads/the-confidences-of-jill-jones
   .2467473.

10. Michael Hamm, "How we made Prince's Purple Rain," *Guardian*, July 24,
    2017, https://www.theguardian.com/music/2017/jul/24/how-we-made
    -princes-purple-rain-interview.

11. Hamm, "How we made Prince's Purple Rain."

12. Dave Lifton, "The Prince album credit that left Wendy and Lisa 'broken-
    hearted,'" *Ultimate Prince*, August 29, 2020, https://ultimateprince.com
    /wendy-lisa-prince-sign-o-the-times.

13. Claire Hoffman, "Prince's Life as a Jehovah's Witness: His Complicated and Ever-Evolving Faith," *Hollywood Reporter*, April 28, 2016, https://www.hollywoodreporter.com/news/music-news/princes-life-as-a-jehovahs-888584. Six years later, Prince had a change of heart, and they did play on the same stage; however, most of their outside work has been writing music for film and television.

14. Claire Hoffman, "Soup with Prince," *New Yorker*, November 16, 2008, https://www.newyorker.com/magazine/2008/11/24/soup-with-prince. Prince tried to walk back his comments a little after the piece was published, and conveniently he did not allow Hoffman to record their interview. However, she stands by her account, saying that she spent an hour in her car immediately afterward, memorializing everything he said. Prince's defenders point to his sizable gay following to argue that he couldn't possibly be homophobic, but note that many of Morrisey's fans don't share his politics, same for Van Morrison, Eric Clapton, and others. Michelle Shocked, once a lesbian icon, reemerged as an avowed homophobe. For a recap, see Daniel Kusner, "Dallas-born alt-rocker Michelle Shocked makes few apologies for 'epic exploit,'" *Dallas Morning News*, July 1, 2017, https://www.dallasnews.com/arts-entertainment/performing-arts/2017/07/01/dallas-born-alt-rocker-michelle-shocked-makes-few-apologies-for-epic-exploit.

15. This happens at about 25:00, https://www.youtube.com/watch?v=pUVZW6-rZKw.

16. Sinéad O'Connor on Norwegian radio, Aoife Kelly, "'I told him to f*** off' — Sinead O'Connor reveals she had punch-up with Prince," *Independent*, November 18, 2014, https://www.independent.ie/entertainment/music/music-news/i-told-him-to-f-off-Sinéad-oconnor-reveals-she-had-punch-up-with-prince-30753189.html.

17. O'Connor told the *Washington Post* that reading the "Prince" chapter of the book for the audio version was retraumatizing. "Transcript: Sinéad O'Connor, Author, 'Rememberings,'" *Washington Post*, June 9, 2021, https://www.washingtonpost.com/washington-post-live/2021/06/09/transcript-sinad-oconnor-author-rememberings.

18. *Hot Press* reported that before launching into his own version of "Nothing Compares 2 U" at a 2012 concert in Kent, Prince told the audience, "I didn't write that song, that's Sinéad O'Connor's. I bought me a house with that song!" "Fachtna O Ceallaigh On Split With Sinéad," *Hot Press*, May 7, 2012, https://www.hotpress.com/music/fachtna-o-ceallaigh-on-split-with-sinead-8901954.

Hurt People Hurt

1. "Sinead O'Connor Opens Up on Mental Illness After Found Safe in Chicago Suburb," *NBC News*, May 16, 2016, https://www.nbcchicago.com/news/local/sinead-oconnor-writes-angry-facebook-post-after-going-missing-in-chicago-suburb/58471.

2. Brittany Spanos, "Arsenio Hall Sues Sinead O'Connor for $5 Million," *Rolling Stone*, May 5, 2016, https://www.rollingstone.com/music/music-news/arsenio-hall-sues-sinead-oconnor-for-5-million-95310. e

3. Aodhan O'Faolain, "Sinéad O'Connor being sued for €500,000 by former manager," *Irish Times*, July 27, 2017, https://www.irishtimes.com/news/crime-and-law/courts/high-court/sinéad-o-connor-being-sued-for-500-000-by-former-manager-1.3168826. That matter was privately settled in 2019.

4. For more on O'Connor's tax debt, Ed Carty, "Sinead O'Connor named as tax defaulter — and makes large settlement," *Independent*, September 27, 2016, https://www.independent.ie/irish-news/sinead-oconnor-named-as-tax-defaulter-and-makes-large-settlement-35083213.html; and selling her home, Sharon McGowan, "Sinead O'Connor sells her Irish home after being handed €160,000 tax bill," *Irish Mirror*, January 3, 2017, https://www.irishmirror.ie/showbiz/irish-showbiz/sinead-oconnor-sells-irish-home-9553680.

5. For more on selling back her master recordings, Jem Aswad, "Reservoir Strikes Deal for Chrysalis Records, Blue Raincoat Music," *Variety*, August 29, 2019, https://variety.com/2019/biz/news/reservoir-strikes-deal-for-chrysalis-records-blue-raincoat-music-1203318874.

6. Sinéad O'Connor, *Rememberings* (New York: HarperCollins, 2021), 269–274.

7. On *Dr. Phil* she explained why she ripped up the photo of the Pope. "Why Sinead O'Connor Says She Ripped Up a Picture of the Pope on Live TV," September 12, 2017, https://www.youtube.com/watch?v=pkumnOW1xRk.

Truthful Witness

1. Andrew Trendell, "Sinead O'Connor Says She Never Wants to Spend Time with White People Again," *NME*, November 6, 2018, https://www.nme.com/news/music/sinead-oconnor-says-never-wants-spend-time-white-people-2397624.

2. For example, see Aidin Vaziri, "Sinéad O'Connor proves value of restraint in comeback," *Datebook*, February 8, 2020, https://datebook.sfchronicle.com/music/review-Sinéad-oconnor-fends-off-controversy-on-her-comeback-tour; Peter Larsen, "Sinéad O'Connor stuns in her first

Southern California show in 8 years," *Orange County Register*, February 12, 2020, https://www.ocregister.com/2020/02/09/sinead-oconnor-stuns-in -her-first-southern-california-show-in-8-years; and Kitty Empire, "Sinéad O'Connor review — still nothing compares," *Guardian*, December 21, 2019, https://www.theguardian.com/music/2019/dec/21/sinead-oconnor-o2 -sheperds-bush-empire-review.

3. For the best audio quality, remote interview subjects are asked to self-record their side of the conversation, which we patch together in post-production so it sounds like we're in the same studio.

4. Sinéad O'Connor, *Rememberings* (New York: HarperCollins, 2021), 181.